Popular Mechanics

Lathe Fundamentals

Rick Peters

Hearst Books

A Division of Sterling Publishing Co., Inc.

New York

Production Staff

Design: Triad Design Group

Cover Design: Margaret Rubiano

Photography: Christopher J. Vendetta

Contributing Writer: Cheryl A. Romano

Cover Photos: Christopher J. Vendetta

Illustrations: Triad Design Group

Copy Editor: Barbara McIntosh Webb

Page Layout: Triad Design Group

Index: Nan Badgett

Library of Congress Cataloging-in-Publication Data Available.

10 9 8 7 6 5 4 3 2 1

Published by Hearst Books
A Division of Sterling Publishing Co., Inc.
387 Park Avenue South, New York, NY 10016

Popular Mechanics is a trademark owned by Hearst Magazines Property, Inc., in USA, and Hearst Communications, Inc., in Canada. Hearst Books is a trademark owned by Hearst Communications, Inc.

www.popularmechanics.com

For information about custom editions, special sales, premium and corporate purchases, please contact Sterling Special Sales Department at 800-805-5489 or specialsales@sterlingpub.com.

Distributed in Canada by Sterling Publishing
C/o Canadian Manda Group, 165 Dufferin Street
Toronto, Ontario, Canada M6K 3H6

Distributed in Australia by Capricorn Link (Australia) Pty. Ltd.,
P.O. Box 704, Windsor, NSW 2756 Australia

Printed in China
All Rights Reserved

ISBN 1-58816-447-0

Contents

ACKNOWLEDGMENTS

For all their help, advice, and support, I offer thanks to:

Canthea McQuoid at Teknatool International for providing the outstanding Nova DVR Lathe, fine Teknatool chucks and accessories, and technical assistance.

Charlotte Gandy at Crown Hand Tools Ltd. for supplying premier lathe tools and technical assistance.

Chad Corley from Delta Machinery for providing two hard-working Delta lathes and technical assistance.

Stephen Feringa of Oneway Manufacturing for the firm's impressive tools and accessories, like their Easy-Core coring system and Wolverine sharpening jig, and technical assistance.

Andrew Greensted of Record Power Ltd. for supplying top-quality lathe tools, and technical assistance.

Christopher Vendetta, for taking great photographs under less-than-desirable conditions and under tight deadlines.

Rob Lembo and the crew at Triad Design Group, for superb illustrations and layout skills, whose talents are evident on every page of this book.

Barb Webb, copyediting whiz, for ferreting out mistakes and gently suggesting corrections.

Heartfelt thanks to my constant inspiration: Cheryl, Lynne, Will, and Liz.

INTRODUCTION

The wood lathe is one of the most underrated stationary tools in the woodshop. It's commonly one of the last big tools that many woodworkers purchase. That's too bad, because adding a lathe to the shop will open up a whole new world of possibilities for your projects. Not only can you embellish projects with turned parts, you can build entire projects on the lathe, like a child's rocker, or a clothes tree, or a round table. But what really sets the lathe apart from other tools is twofold. No other power tool allows you to start and finish the project on the same tool—and in some cases in just a matter of minutes (like a turned pen). Chuck a rough blank in between the centers, shape, and sand it, and then apply a finish to the project—all on the lathe.

What's more, we've always felt that the wood lathe really gets the creative juices flowing. No other power tool promotes creativity like the wood lathe. Our photographer, Chris, calls the lathe "a pottery wheel for wood." It allows you to shape wood in myriad forms unattainable with any other power tool: vases, platters, bowls, hollow vessels, and free-form sculpture. You can chuck up a bit of wood and just make shavings if you want. We often will turn a few quick projects on the lathe in between challenging or complicated furniture projects, just to enjoy the freedom the lathe offers and to see a project shape up right before our eyes in minutes.

If you haven't turned, we wholeheartedly urge you to give it a try. Some woodworkers get so enamored with turning that they virtually give up all other woodworking to concentrate solely on turning. For some, the lathe is the tool they've been waiting for—in particular, those who have felt restricted by the fractions of an inch required for furniture construction. They really enjoy a tool that lets them shape at will.

We hope you'll give turning a try and are sure you'll enjoy letting those shavings fly as much as we do.

—James Miegs

Editor-in-Chief, **Popular Mechanics**

1 Choosing a Lathe

Lathe users generally fall into one of two broad categories: the occasional turner and the turning enthusiast. Occasional turners will use a lathe to make parts for a furniture project (like spindles for a rocking chair) and to turn simple projects for gifts, etc. For turning enthusiasts, the lathe is their primary tool; the bulk of their time in the shop will be spent working on the lathe to turn platters, bowls, and one-of-a-kind pieces. The type of turner you are will define what type of lathe is best for you.

Like all other power tools, there are numerous lathes to choose from. Each can be loosely classified as stationary (or floor model), bench-top, midi, or mini-lathe. So how do you choose the lathe that's right for you? You start by learning all you can about the different types of lathes and their features. That's what this chapter is all about. We'll take you through the basics and show what features to look for, and what to look out for. We'll cover power and lathe capacities along with things like Morse tapers and tool rest adjustments that can make using a lathe a joy or a chore. Armed with this information, you'll be able to choose a lathe that meets your needs—either as an occasional turner or as a turning enthusiast, or both.

Lathes come in four basic sizes: stationary, bench-top, midi, and mini. The size that's best for you will depend primarily on the type of work you do now and in the future. The Nova DVR 3000 lathe shown here blurs the line between stationary and bench-top; although it fits on a bench top, it has the power and capacity of some stationary lathes.

Stationary Lathe

Unless you're turning professionally, are wealthy, or just like large tools, it's hard for the average woodworker to justify the expense of a large stationary lathe like the one shown in the top photo. Granted, these are the smoothest-running, largest-capacity lathes out there. But for most woodworkers, there's little reason to buy a lathe this big unless you want to specialize in large bowls or hollow vessels. These beefy machines feature a stand, bed, and parts made from heavy cast iron. The swing (twice the distance between the headstock spindle and the lathe bed—or the largest-diameter blank the lathe can handle) varies between 12" and 25". The between-centers capacity of these lathes (the longest blank the lathe can handle) runs from 16" up to 120" (that's 10 feet!). The motors are often 2-hp and larger, with variable speeds. These industrial-strength lathes often tip the scales at $1/4$ to $1/2$ ton. The price tag is also hefty—anywhere from $2,000 to $5,000.

Big and expensive, yes—but a lathe like this is a joy to use. Because of the massive castings, vibration is near nonexistent. You can chuck a huge bowl blank up and turn it with ease. Additionally, most stationary lathe manufacturers offer exceptional accessories for their lathes, like Oneway's Easy-Core system and their deep hollowing system. The Easy-Core system allows you to literally scoop out the interiors of bowls in one piece for use as future bowls instead of turning this wood into shavings. The deep hollowing system lets you hollow out deep vessels with relative ease.

TYPICAL STATIONARY LATHE

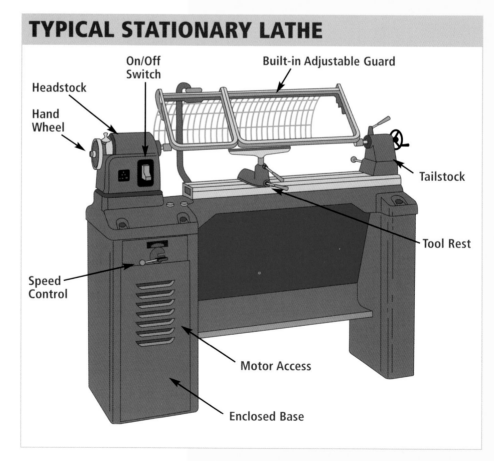

On/Off Switch

Built-in Adjustable Guard

Headstock

Hand Wheel

Tailstock

Tool Rest

Speed Control

Motor Access

Enclosed Base

Bench-Top Lathe

In most cases, a bench-top lathe is all the lathe the average woodworker will need in the shop. Bench-top lathes can be mounted to a workbench or other stand, but many now come with a set of legs or a metal stand like the one shown in the bottom left drawing. This type of lathe will usually come with a 3/4-hp or 1-hp motor—plenty of power for most turning tasks. Typical swing for a bench-top lathe can vary between 8" and 16", with 12" being the most common. Between-centers capacity can be anywhere from 12" to 42", with 36" the most common. A bench-top lathe can be had for as little as $350, or you can pay well over $1,000.

As you'll discover when you read on, the line between lathe types is getting blurry. Many lathe manufacturers are introducing bench-top lathes with features and capacities that rival the larger, more costly stationary lathes. Optional accessories, like Nova's bed extensions, allow you to increase the bed width from the standard 24" up to an impressive 44". And by adding a motor swivel (page 18) that allows you to turn outboard, the swing of the lathe is greatly increased (for more on lathe capacities, see page 14).

TYPICAL BENCH-TOP LATHE

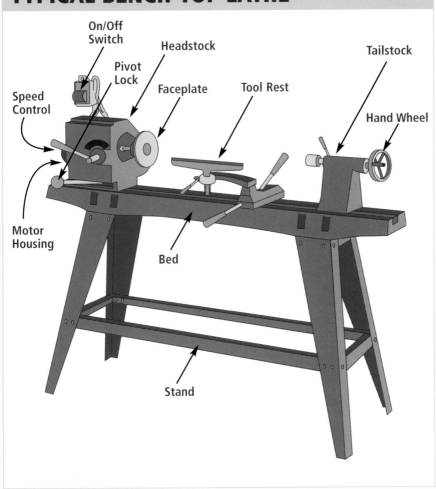

On/Off Switch

Headstock

Tailstock

Pivot Lock

Faceplate

Tool Rest

Hand Wheel

Speed Control

Motor Housing

Bed

Stand

Midi Lathe

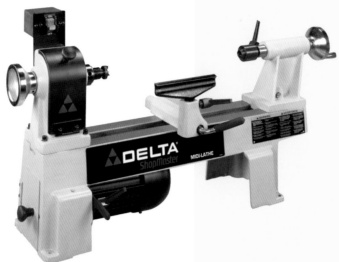

A number of years ago, savvy lathe makers realized that there was a significant gap between the capacities of bench-top lathes and mini-lathes. Many woodworkers didn't want to invest the shop space and money for a bench-top lathe but were unsatisfied with the abilities of the much smaller mini-lathes. This spurred the birth of what are now commonly called midi lathes. Although these lathes are smaller than bench-top lathes, they're considerably heavier and bulkier than mini lathes. Most midi lathes come with a ¹/₂-hp motor and have a swing ranging from 8" to 10". Between-centers capacity is still fairly limited, however—commonly 11" to 15". Some lathes, like the Delta midi shown here, accept bed extensions to provide between-centers capacity of 37", comparable to many bench-top lathes.

The big difference here, however, is the beefiness of the castings. The stouter bed allows for turning larger, heavier blanks without fear of lathe damage. Many of these when bolted to a sturdy stand will handle most turning tasks for the average woodworker, and they're hundreds of dollars less expensive then their larger bench-top cousins.

TYPICAL MIDI LATHE

On/Off Switch

Headstock

Drive Center

Hand Wheel

Hand Wheel

Tailstock

Belt Access

Base

Motor

Tool Rest

Mini-Lathe

Mini-lathes have been around for a number of years now and have become popularized by an easy-to-make and enjoyable project—turned pens. These diminutive lathes really are smaller versions of midi lathes (typically weighing half as much as a midi) and are light enough that you can pick them up and store them away when not in use. Typical motor sizes are $1/4$, $1/3$, and $1/2$ hp, with $1/2$ hp being the most common. Bed swing is typically 6", but some are available with an 8" swing. You'll really notice the "mini" part when it comes to between-centers capacity: Common capacities are 8" to 12". This limits the usefulness of this type of lathe to small projects like pens, brackets, tops, wine stoppers, and small plates and shallow bowls.

Even if you bolt one of these lathes down to a sturdy base, don't try turning large blanks on them. The castings are just not designed to handle the stress, and you can rack the bed out of alignment quite easily—especially if the blank you're turning is out of balance.

TYPICAL MINI-LATHE

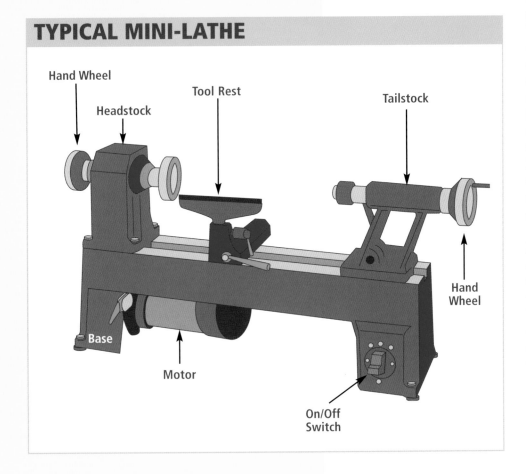

- Hand Wheel
- Headstock
- Tool Rest
- Tailstock
- Hand Wheel
- Base
- Motor
- On/Off Switch

Specialty Lathes

In addition to the standard lathes we've already discussed, there are a couple of specialty lathes you may want to consider before purchasing a lathe, depending on what type of work you plan to do.

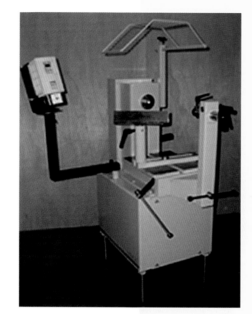

Bowl-turning lathe

Anyone who's ever turned a bowl on a conventional lathe knows that the stance you take to turn can be quite awkward. That is, you have to bend over the bed to see what you're turning. Not only is this uncomfortable, but it's also dangerous. If what you want to turn is bowls, consider a bowl lathe like the Vega lathe shown in the top photo. The advantage of a bowl lathe is that you can stand directly in front of the lathe while you turn. Better stance, better access, and safer—particularly for larger bowls. The disadvantage of this type of lathe is that it has no tailstock and therefore you can't turn between centers—something that is quite limiting for all-around use.

Pen-turning lathe

If shop space is really confined and you'd like to concentrate on pen turning, some manufacturers have produced lathes with this in mind. The tiny Jet pen lathe shown in the middle photo is one example of this. Although severely limited in capacity, this lathe is so small you can take with you on a vacation or other trip.

LATHE DUPLICATORS

If you're thinking about a project that calls for a lot of identical parts—like spindles for a baby's crib—consider a lathe duplicator. Although there are duplicating lathes, these are primarily used for mass production in the furniture and accessories industries. A less expensive alternative is to purchase a duplicator accessory for your lathe. We mention this here because not all lathes offer this accessory, and if you plan on ever doing repetitive work, it's worth your time now to identify which lathes offer duplicators. These accessories basically bolt to your lathe. A finger on the duplicator follows your pattern (the part you're duplicating) and controls a cutter that duplicates this pattern on a blank. The duplicating process can be slow and the turning often comes out rough, as the cutter is basically a scraper, but you can't beat its ability to replicate parts.

Lathe Motors

Unlike many stationary tools where the tool is basically defined by the motor size, lathes are usually classified as to their capacities, as described on page 14. That's not to say motor size and type are not important for a lathe—they are. A couple of motor specs to look for when comparing lathes are: Is the lathe belt-driven or direct-drive? And is motor speed variable in increments or is it continuously variable?

Belt-driven

The headstocks on most lathes are driven by the motor via a belt and a set of pulleys (left photo). In most cases, this type of drive system works just fine as long as belt tension is correct and the cut is controlled. The disadvantage to this type of drive is that belt slippage is common. This can make it difficult to control the lathe tool while turning. But this disadvantage can also be a plus when a catch occurs—basically when either a tool is introduced to the spinning wood improperly or the cut is too deep. When a catch occurs with a small motor, the blank will often stop spinning and the belt will simply slip continuously on the pulley. With stronger motors, this may not occur and a catch can be nasty situation.

Direct-drive

Innovative lathe manufacturers like Teknatool, manufacturers of Nova lathes, have introduced lathes that are direct-drive—no belts to slip (top right photo). With a direct-drive lathe, the motor drives the headstock directly, which is enclosed in the same unit as the motor. Not only does this eliminate belt slippage and maintenance, but it also allows for advanced technology. Teknatool offers one version of their direct-drive lathes with a feature called digital

variable reluctance (DVR). Basically, an on-board computer senses the drag on the workpiece when cutting and adjusts speed and torque to provide a controlled cut. For more on DVR technology, go to www.teknatool.com.

Incremental speeds

Most belt-driven lathes provide a number of speeds in set increments, typically around six speeds. To change speed, you have to stop the lathe, loosen the belt tension, and physically move the belt from step pulley to step pulley (middle right photo). Then readjust the belt tension and you're ready to go. A bit of an inconvenience, yes, but this helps keep costs down. At minimum, we think you should have five speeds, with the lowest around 350 rpm.

Continuously variable

Deluxe lathes offer true variable speed, typically from 0 to 2,500 rpm. But be warned that this feature is expensive—it can easily add $250 to $500 to the cost of the lathe. Speed changes can be made manually (like shifting the lever on the lathe shown in the bottom right photo), or by adjusting an electronic control or touchpad, as is the case with the Nova lathe shown above.

Lathe Beds

Besides the horsepower rating of a lathe, the two most common specifications you'll want to check into are its working capacities—particularly the bed length or "working distance between centers" and the bed depth or "swing over tool rest." These two specifications will tell you the maximum size workpiece that the lathe can safely handle.

Bed length

Bed length, or working distance between centers, is a fairly straightforward specification. It basically defines the distance between the headstock center and the tailstock center. Note that some lathe manufacturers offer extensions for their beds.

Bed depth

Bed depth, or swing over tool rest (also called swing over bed), can be a bit confusing. Technically, the bed depth is the distance between the drive center and the bed (bottom left drawing). But this number is rarely given. Instead manufacturers double this and call it bed swing. To add to the confusion, some man-

ufacturers create a notch in the bed known as a recessed bed to increase the swing (bottom right drawing). It's important to note that this only increases the swing at the notch—this is fine for turning platters and shallow bowls, but has no effect on spindle-turning capacity.

Bed styles

There are three common bed styles available ranging from good to practically useless. At the useless end of the scale are stamped metal beds shaped into square rails. This type of bed does not offer the weight or rigidity that the headstock and tailstock need—the result is a machine that often vibrates so badly that turning is dangerous. Another weak system is a single hollow tube. This also lacks the necessary weight and rigidity. The best beds are made with twin solid metal bars (right photo) or from thick cast iron (top photo). Both are heavy and rigid and do a great job of dampening vibration.

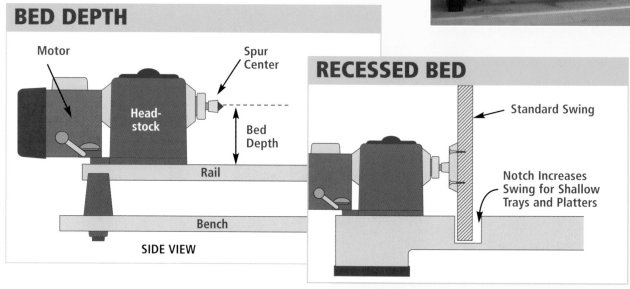

BED DEPTH

Motor · Spur Center · Head-stock · Bed Depth · Rail · Bench · SIDE VIEW

RECESSED BED

Standard Swing · Notch Increases Swing for Shallow Trays and Platters

MORSE TAPER ANATOMY

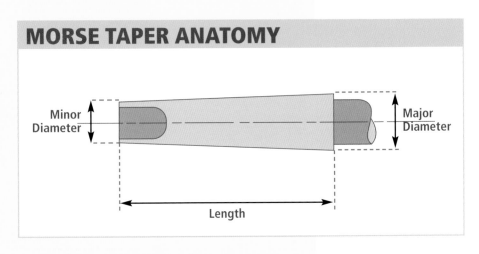

Minor Diameter

Major Diameter

Length

Morse Tapers

The headstock and tailstock splindles on a lathe are hollow to accept the centers. Both the spindle holes and the centers are tapered to create a snug, friction fit between the parts. The size of the hole and its taper are defined by the Morse taper method—a system used by machinists to describe a cone within a cone. Morse taper sizes range from #1 to #7; see the chart below and the top drawing. You'll find most lathes use either a #1 or #2 Morse taper. You should know that a #2 Morse taper is more common and that you'll find more accessories designed for this versus the #1. You may occasionally come across a #3MT, but these are fairly rare except on larger lathes. Please note that Morse taper adapters are available from most mail-order turning catalogs, but they're designed only to adapt smaller centers to fit machines with larger tapers.

TAPER EXTENSIONS

You might occasionally encounter a turning situation where you wish one of your Morse tapers were longer than it is. A good example of this is when coring with the Oneway Easy-Core system as described on pages 88–91. Because of the system, your tailstock can't reach the workpiece to support it while coring. Here's where a taper extension comes in handy (bottom left photo). You can use one to extend the tailstock center over to the workpiece as shown in the bottom photo on page 89. Taper extensions are available for most taper sizes and can be found wherever machinist's supplies are sold.

MORSE TAPER SPECIFICATIONS

Morse Number	Taper*	Minor Diameter	Major Diameter	Length
0	0.05205	0.252"	0.3561"	2.000"
1	0.04988	0.369"	0.4750"	1.126"
2	0.04995	0.572"	0.700"	2.562"
3	0.05019	0.778"	0.938"	3.188"
4	0.05193	1.020"	1.231"	4.064"
5	0.05262	1.475"	1.748"	5.188"
6	0.05213	2.116"	2.494"	7.252"
7	0.05200	2.750"	3.270"	10.00"

*Diameter in inches per inch of length

Lathe Fit and Finish

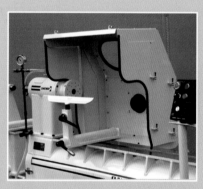

As you begin to narrow down your lathe choices, one thing that we always recommend you do is get your hands on the tools you're considering. Whether this means a trip to the tool store, to a woodworking show, or to a friend's shop, take the time to see and feel these tools.

Castings and machining

One thing you'll never find out about from a website or a catalog is the fit and finish of the lathe. Fit and finish will say a lot about how the lathe is put together. We're talking about quality of castings and machined surfaces. In general, a lathe with rough castings and poorly machined surfaces (top right photo) will be of lesser quality than a lathe with clean castings and smooth surfaces (top left photo). Much of this has to do with the philosophy of the lathe manufacturer. In particular, "Can we get by with this?" versus "Let's do it right." Inspect all the surfaces of the lathe, including the headstock, tailstock, bed, tool rest, and stand. The better the castings and machining, the odds are the higher the quality of the lathe.

SPECIALTY FEATURES

There are a couple of specialty features that we've really come to appreciate in a lathe. These are the kind of features that, once you get used to them, you'll wonder how you ever did without them before. In particular: indexing, hollow drilling, and a functional dust hood.

Indexing. All quality lathes offer some kind of indexing of the headstock spindle; that is, a way to lock it in place in one or more positions. At minimum, you should be able to lock the spindle to make accessory changing easier. Deluxe lathes will offer multiple stops or indexes so that you can rotate and stop the headstock at set intervals. The Nova lathe shown here indexes the spindle in 15-degree increments. This is particularly useful if you embellish your turnings by carving flutes, etc., on the spindle surface.

Hollow drilling. The spindles on most tailstocks are hollow so that you can readily remove the tailstock center by tapping it with a metal rod. Some lathe manufacturers offer bushings that allow you to drill through the tailstock directly into the workpiece. This is especially useful for drilling long holes through spindles, as is the case when making a lamp.

Dust hood. Most beginning turners are unaware of how much dust and debris can be generated by even a small turning. Turning larger objects (like bowls) can leave you surrounded by shavings. A good dust hood can minimize this. None of the hoods we've used capture all the dust and shavings, but any help here is better than none.

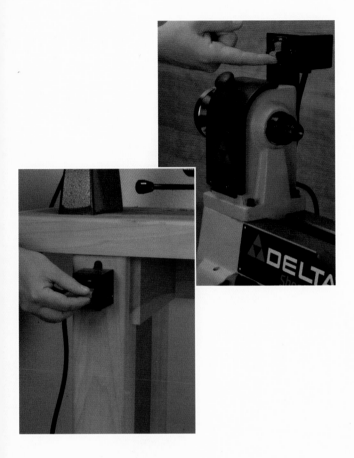

Ergonomics

In addition to visiting a tool store or show to check out a lathe's fit and finish, this is also an excellent opportunity to get a feel for the lathe's ergonomics—that is, the position and operation of the various controls and adjustments. Manually operate each of the following: switches, adjustment knobs, spindle lock, motor swivel (if applicable), headstock, tailstock, and tool rest.

Power switch

The location and ease of use of a lathe's power switch is hugely important as you'll be constantly turning the lathe on and off—more so than any other stationary power tool you use. That's why it's imperative that the switch be located within easy reach (top photo). The last thing you want to be doing is bending over to toggle a hard-to-reach switch (far left photo). If possible, look for a switch that offers a large paddle-type switch that can be turned off with an elbow or knee if needed.

Adjustment knobs and levers

Although it might seem like a small detail, the types and locations of adjustment knobs and levers on the lathe (particularly on the tool rest) can be a blessing or a curse. Avoid (or consider replacing) knobs that aren't spring-loaded. Spring-loaded knobs (bottom left photo) allow you to push in the knob and spin it out of the way once the tool rest is locked in place. This is important if you want to avoid constantly having to reposition the tool rest. Activate each knob and lever and check to see if it interferes with other lathe parts or knobs. The clamp lever on the tool rest in the bottom right photo interferes with the arms of the tool rest and will be a constant aggravation in use.

Spindle lock

Since most turners use the spindle lock all the time to lock the spindle in order to change accessories (like chucks, faceplates, etc.), the location and ease of use of the spindle lock is important. Many lathes have the spindle lock on the end of the lathe and you need to reach around to engage/disengage the lock. A better location is on top of the headstock, like the Nova lathe shown in the top photo.

Motor pivot

Some lathes offer a pivoting headstock that allows you to rotate the headstock 90 degrees in order to turn large workpieces as shown in the middle photo. The type and detent on the lock will affect how easy it is to use and how well it performs. If you're purchasing a lathe with a pivoting headstock, rotate the headstock into its outboard position and lock it in place. Then try and move it by twisting the headstock—it shouldn't budge. If it does, the lock is ineffective, and outboard turning will be sloppy at best and hazardous at worst.

Headstock

The headstock of a lathe you're considering is worthy of some serious attention. Check to see how well it's secured to the bed, and whether it's designed to move or pivot (see above). Stay away from spindles that are supported by ball bearings—they just don't hold up over time and often introduce a huge amount of play. Better yet, look for a lathe that uses roller bearings. These long, cylindrical bearings are better suited to support the spindle while minimizing play. Additionally, look for stout, heavy castings that are well machined (bottom left photo), versus lightweight castings (bottom right photo).

Tailstock

Almost equally important as the headstock on a lathe is the tailstock: It supports the opposite end of the workpiece and must be rigid enough to suppress vibration, but also must have a locking mechanism that lets you move it easily yet will still lock it firmly in place. There are three common controls on a tailstock: the clamp lock that locks the tailstock in place on the lathe bed, a wheel that lets you adjust the tailstock center in and out, and a lock that freezes the tailstock in place at the desired location. Besides having easy-to-use knobs and levers (preferably, the spring-loaded variety), make sure the wheel has a rotating knob or lever so you can spin the wheel quickly (top left photo) versus having to rotate the wheel by hand (top right photo).

Tool rest

The tool rest is the number one most adjusted part of a lathe. You will be constantly adjusting and readjusting its position as you turn to compensate for wood removed and to better control cuts. The typical tool rest has two adjustments: a clamp to lock the base of the tool rest in place, and typically a spring-loaded lever that is used to simultaneously adjust the height and angle of the tool rest with respect to the workpiece. Since you'll be moving and adjusting the tool rest continually, look for a unit that slides easily on the lathe bed, locks firmly in position (bottom left photo), and has knobs that don't interfere with each other, as shown in the bottom right photo.

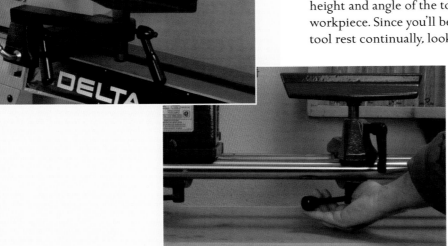

■ RECOMMENDATIONS

Unless you're a production turner, we recommend a bench-top lathe. Look for a cast iron or solid metal bar bed, pivoting head-stock, and at least five speeds. If at all possible, visit a tool center or woodworking show to get your hands on the lathes you're interested in. Also, there are a number of woodworking user groups on the web where you can read about turners' reactions to lathes. On the other hand, if you're looking only to turn small projects, a midi or mini-lathe is a good choice. The only complaint we've heard from turners about these is they often exceed the lathe's capacities and wish they'd invested in a bench-top lathe from the start.

MIDI/MINI LATHES

Brand/Model	Motor (rpm)	Speeds	Range	Swing	Between Centers	Spindle & Taper	Weight (lbs.)
Carba-tec 4SE	¼ hp	variable	400–4500	6"	12½"	¾" 16 tpi MT#1	37
Craftsman 21708	60 watts	3	1300–3000	4"	12"	MT#1	10
Delta LA200	½ hp	6	500–3700	10"	14½"–37"	1" 8 tpi MT#2	85
Fisch	½ hp	6	500–3700	10"	15"	1" 8 tpi MT#2	85
General 25-100 M1	½ hp	6	480–4023	10"	15"	1" 8 tpi MT#2	106
Grizzly G8690	⅓ hp	variable	0–3025	6¼"	20"	MT#1	40
Grizzly G9247	¼ hp	variable	300–4750	5⁵⁄₁₆"	12"	MT#1	46
Jet JML-1014K	½ hp	6	500–3975	10"	14"	1" 8 tpi MT#2	69
Nova Mercury	¼ hp	3 ranges	100–3800	8"	11"	1" 8 tpi MT#2	59
Turncrafter Plus	¼ hp	variable	750–3200	7½"	12½"	¾" 16 tpi MT#1	43
Turncrafter Pro	½ hp	5	500–3200	10"	18"–40"	1" 8 tpi MT#2	68–87

BENCH-TOP LATHES

Brand/Model	Motor (rpm)	Speeds	Range	Swing	Between Centers	Spindle & Taper	Weight (lbs.)
Craftsman 21712	5.5 amps	variable	380–2150	12"	36"	MT#2	155
Craftsman 21715	1 hp	variable	0–2150	15"	38"	MT#2	175
Delta 46-715	¾ hp	variable	500–2500	14"	40"	1" 8 tpi MT#2	300
General 160-1	¾ hp	6	600–2800	16"	38"	1¼" 8 tpi MT#2	283
General 160-2	¾ or 1 hp	variable	375–3300	24½"	38"	1¼" 8 tpi MT#2	339
Nova 3000	1 hp	8 or variable	178–3000	16"	24"–44"	1¼" 8 tpi MT#2	145
Oneway 1018	1 hp	3 ranges	0–4000	10	18"–42"	1" 8 tpi MT#2	280
Grizzly G5979	½" hp	10	580–2850	12"	35½"	MT#2	190
Grizzly G1067Z	½" hp	6	510–2800	14"	40"	1" 12 tpi MT#2	190
Jet JWL-1236	¾ hp	6	550–3000	8¾"	34½"	1" 8 tpi MT#2	183
Jet JWL-1442	1 hp	8	450–3000	10"	42"	1" 8 tpi MT#2	190
Jet JWL-1642	1½ or 2 hp	variable	0–3200	12"	42"	1¼" 8 tpi MT#2	410
Oneway 1224	1 hp	2 ranges	0–4500	12"	24"–48"	1" 8 tpi MT#2	300
Record DML24X-MK2	⅓ hp	4	450–2000	9"	24"	¾" 16 tpi MT#?	88
Record DML36SH-MK2	⅓ hp	4	450–2000	9"	36"	¾" 16 tpi MT#?	90
Record CL3	¾ hp	5	425–2000	12"	36"	¾" 16 tpi MT#?	190
Shopsmith Mark V	13.5 amps	variable	700–5200	16½"	34"	MT#2	210

STATIONARY LATHES

Brand/Model	Motor (rpm)	Speeds	Range	Swing	Between Centers	Spindle & Taper	Weight (lbs.)
Delta 46-756	2 hp	variable	0–3000	16"	42"	1¼" 8 tpi MT#2	430
General 260	1 hp	4 or variable	600–2800, 375–3300	12"	38"–98"	1¼" 8 tpi MT#2	524
General 26020	2 hp	4 or variable	375–3300, 600, 1050, 1720, 2800	20"	38"–98"	1¼" 8 tpi MT#2	542
General 260VD	2 hp	variable and reversible	0–3000	12"	38"–98"	1¼" 8 tpi MT#2	544
Grizzly G1495	¾ hp	7	500–3070	14"	40"	1" 12 tpi MT#2	262
Powermatic 3520	2 or 3 hp	2 ranges	0–1200, 0–3200	16"	34½"	1¼" 8 tpi MT#2	717
Powermatic 4224	3 hp	3 ranges	0–910, 0–2000, 0–3500	18½"	42"	1¼" 8 tpi MT#2	891
Oneway 1640	1½ or 2 hp	2 ranges	14–700, 51–2500	12¼"	40"	M33¥3.5 MT#2	600
Oneway 2016	1½, 2 or 3 hp	variable and reversible	0–3000	15"	16"	M33¥3.5 MT#2	600
Oneway 2036	1½, 2 or 3 hp	variable and reversible	0–3000	15"	36"	M33¥3.5 MT#2	800
Oneway 2416	1½, 2 or 3 hp	variable and reversible	0–3000	19"	16"	M33¥3.5 MT#2	650
Oneway 2436	1½, 2, or 3 hp	variable and reversible	0–3000	19"	36"	M33¥3.5 MT#2	850
Serious SL2536	3 hp	2 ranges	25–900 & 100–3650	25"	36"	1½" 8 tpi MT#4	1200
Vega 1500	1½ hp	variable	320–3400	15"	53"–120"	1" 8 tpi MT#2	450–500

BOWL LATHES

Brand/Model	Motor (rpm)	Speeds	Range	Swing	Between Centers	Spindle & Taper	Weight (lbs.)
Serious BL3514	3 hp	2 ranges	10–228 & 200–3650	35"	14"	1½" 8 tpi MT#3	850
VB Manufacturing VB36	2 or 3 hp	3 ranges	50–500, 150–1350, 250–2600	26"	Up to 31"	60¥500mm MT#3	583–689
Vega 24 bowl lathe	¾ hp	4 ranges	200–525, 375–975, 750–1650, 1200–3000	24"	n/a	1" 8 tpi MT#2	160
Vega 2400T bowl lathe	1½ hp AC or DC	2 variable	AC: 160–425 & 800–2200 DC: 0–425 & 0–2520	24"	6"–17"	1¼" 8 tpi MT#2	500

2 Lathe Accessories

By itself, all that any lathe is capable of is spinning a piece of wood. You'll need a variety of accessories to cut and shape the wood. Additionally, you'll likely find that the more you get into turning, the more accessories you'll acquire—particularly those designed to grip wood in different ways.

In this chapter, we'll take you through the most common lathe accessories. Everything from tools for laying out and measuring a blank or workpiece to tools for shaping and cutting, as well as the myriad chucks available for gripping different kinds of work. Along the way, we'll make suggestions on what to look for and some recommendations on specific accessories that we found particularly noteworthy. By the end of the chapter you should have enough information to comfortably choose just the right accessories for your upcoming lathe projects.

To shape and hold wood in a lathe, you'll need a number of accessories, including marking and measuring tools, turning tools, and a variety of chucks.

Measuring and Marking

There are a couple of specialty layout tools that every turner will want to have on hand: calipers and center finders. Calipers are designed to let you quickly check the diameter of a part or portion of a turning. Center finders make finding the center of a blank quick and easy.

Calipers

At first glance, many calipers look just like a set of dividers or a compass. On closer examination you'll find that the difference lies in the legs. On a set of inside calipers, the legs bow out at the tips (left calipers in drawing below); with outside calipers, they curve gently in at the ends (right calipers in drawing below). Calipers are used to take accurate inside and outside measurements so that these can be transferred to another layout or can be reproduced. A transfer caliper is a special caliper that has a secondary leg that can be locked in position once the measurement has been taken. This allows you to either open or close the caliper without losing the measurement. A final type of caliper is the double-ended caliper (far left in left photo). One end is clamped over the part to be measured, and you can measure the gap at the opposite end while the caliper is still in place.

Center markers

Finding the center of a blank is a common task prior to turning. It's so common that a number of tool manufacturers make plastic and metal center find-

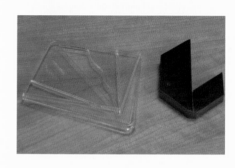

ers like the ones shown in the photo above. Either type of center finder has lips (or edges) on two adjacent sides to position the workpiece. To use a center finder, press the edges of the workpiece up against the lips of the center finder. Then butt a pencil or marking knife up against the center cutout and draw along this to mark a line on the workpiece. Next, rotate the workpiece 90 degrees and make another mark. Where the lines intersect is dead center.

TYPES OF CALIPERS

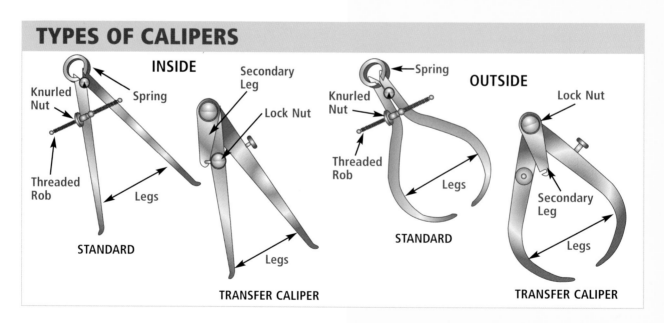

INSIDE

Knurled Nut — Spring — Secondary Leg — Lock Nut — Threaded Rob — Legs — STANDARD — Legs — TRANSFER CALIPER

OUTSIDE

Spring — Knurled Nut — Lock Nut — Threaded Rob — Legs — STANDARD — Secondary Leg — Legs — TRANSFER CALIPER

Lathe Stands

A lathe is only as good as the stand it's on. Although this may seem like an overstatement, it's not. One of the keys to successful turning is a vibration-free lathe. And the secret to dampening vibration is a well-made, stout, and heavy stand. You'll find three basic types available: stamped metal, welded steel, and wood.

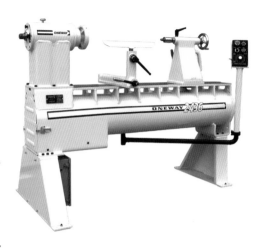

Welded steel

The ultimate in vibration-dampening stands are made of thick plates of steel that are welded together to make a heavy, massive stand like the one shown in the top right photo. Though these can be costly, they are well worth the price, as you'll experience smooth cutting even when turning heavy blanks.

Wood

An inexpensive option is to build your own lathe stand out of wood. The one shown in the photo below has a long shallow box underneath that can be filled with sand or bricks to increase its weight and help dampen vibration. For step-by-step instructions on how to build this lathe stand, see pages 122–129.

Stamped metal

The stands provided by most lathe manufacturers are made from stamped metal. They come unassembled and go together quickly. Although they do a decent job of supporting the lathe, they do little to dampen vibration. If the stand has a lower set of supports like the one shown in the left photo, consider bolting a shelf on top of the supports and then adding some weight in the form of tubes of sand or bricks, as described in the sidebar below.

DAMPENING VIBRATION

The heavier a lathe stand is, the better it can dampen vibration. Any stand can be improved by adding weight to the stand. Two inexpensive options are sand and bricks. Sand tends to work the best, as it fills a box or tray more completely than bricks. Tubes of sand also work well, as you can drape them over stand brackets if necessary. ShopTip: If you're going to fill a wood box or tray with sand, make sure the sand is dry. Bags of sand sold at most home centers are wet and will cause the wood to swell and eventually mold.

Chucks

A lathe chuck is any accessory for the lathe that's designed to grip a workpiece. Common versions include the scroll chuck, screw chuck, and drill chuck. Scroll chucks (also called 4-jaw chucks) have numerous jaw sets available, including: collet jaws, stepped jaws, bowl jaws, cole jaws, and pin jaws. Regardless of the type of chuck and accessory jaws you're using, make sure to consult the owner's manual for the maximum size blank the chuck can handle and maximum safe lathe speed.

Scroll chuck

In our opinion, the scroll chuck, or 4-jaw chuck, is one of the niftiest lathe accessories you can buy (upper left photo). These chucks (often referred to by one of many brand names, such as a Nova chuck, a Vicmarc chuck, or a Oneway Stronghold, Talon, or Scroll chuck) grip a workpiece with four jaws that are tightened with a pair of metal rods or an Allen wrench. Because the jaws are beveled on the ends, they can be used to grip a similarly beveled recess in the bottom of a bowl, platter, or other object. Extremely versatile, these chucks typically cost around $200, and numerous accessory jaws are available (see pages 27–28).

Screw chuck

A screw chuck is a hollow metal cap that threads onto the headstock spindle. A hole in the top center of the cap accepts a screw that passes through it and screws into the work-piece (bottom photo). This type of chuck is particularly useful

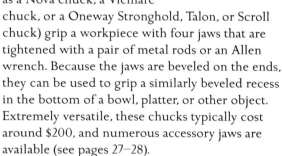

for turning small items such as small lidded boxes. Since the workpiece is held in place only by the screw, it's a good idea to use the tailstock to support the other end while you true up the workpiece. ShopTip: You may find that inserting a strip or two of double-sided tape between the chuck and the workpiece will provide a superior grip and prevent the workpiece from spinning in case of a "catch."

Drill chuck

Another useful chuck accessory for your lathe is a drill chuck (upper right photo). It's basically a drill chuck that fits onto one end of a Morse taper center. You can insert this chuck into the headstock to drive a round workpiece, or use it in the tailstock to hold a drill bit. This is the more common use for a drill chuck, as it excels at drilling a perfectly centered hole in a round workpiece—it's a great way to remove the bulk of the waste from a turned box. And if you use a true Forstner bit, you'll end up with a true flat-bottomed hole.

Spigot jaws

Spigot jaws come in variety of sizes and are designed to powerfully grip one end on an unsupported workpiece like that shown in the top photo. The interior walls of spigot jaws are ribbed to provide a better purchase on a blank. This makes spigot jaws ideal for turning unsupported work like vases, goblets, and small boxes. Although primarily used to grip in the contracting mode, spigot jaws can also be used to grip stock in the expanding mode.

Stepped jaws

Stepped jaws can be a bit confusing because different lathe makers have different ideas of what stepped jaws are used for. Regardless of their intended use, stepped jaws will always have steps machined into the jaws—on either the exterior or interior of the jaws. Jaws with the steps on the exterior (like those shown in the middle photo) are designed to grip the inside of a workpiece—either a recess in the base of a workpiece, or its interior walls. If you turn bowls that are footed—that is, there's a stub or base of the bowl—you can use stepped jaws with steps on the interior of the jaws to grip the foot of the bowl so you can then turn the inside of the bowl. Interior stepped jaws are designed to grip the foot in the contracting mode. The different step sizes will allow you to grip a variety of foot sizes without crushing the wood and damaging the foot.

SPINDLE ADAPTERS

Most savvy accessory manufacturers sell spindle adapters for their chucks. A spindle adapter is basically a machined nut with female threads on the inside and a male threaded stub on the outside, as shown in the bottom photo. To use a spindle adapter, simply screw the adapter onto your lathe spindle and then screw your chuck onto the adapter. Spindle adapters allow the manufacturers to make just a few different sizes of threaded chucks that can fit onto a variety of lathe spindles—you just choose the appropriate adapter. Also, if you're fortunate enough to have more than one lathe in the shop but they have different size spindles, adapters allow you to use one size chuck on both lathes.

Bowl jaws

Bowls jaws are often referred to as power-grip jaws and are intended to support large, long, or heavy workpieces. They can do this because they are much more massive than standard chuck jaws. Compare the thickness and length of the bowl jaws shown in the top photo here with the standard jaws on the chuck shown in the upper left photo on page 26. Beefier jaws mean you can exert more pressure on a workpiece to achieve a better grip.

Cole jaws

Cole jaws are basically flat segments of aluminum that fit onto a scroll chuck and have a series of threaded holes designed to accept rubber bumpers held in place with screws. This setup allows you to rechuck a bowl to remove marks on the bottom of the bowl made by a chuck or faceplate screws. The rubber bumpers are adjusted to accept the bowl, and the chuck is constricted so the bumpers grip the bowl, as shown in the middle photo. It should be noted that cole jaws do not grip a workpiece as firmly as other accessory jaws and it's important to take only light cuts when cleaning up the bottom of the bowl.

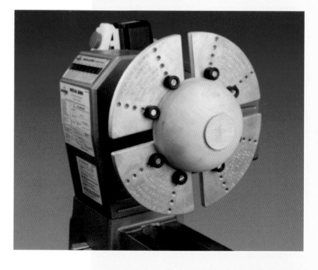

Pin jaws

Pin jaws have much longer tips that, when expanded inside a bored hole, will grip the workpiece securely, as shown in the bottom photo. This is an especially useful technique if you want to create a freeform-edged bowl. What's nice about these jaws is that you don't have to bore an exact-sized hole; the range of adjustment of the chuck will take up any play. Pin jaws can also be used in the contracting mode to grip thin spindle work, such as lace bobbins. You can even mount twist drills in these jaws and use it as a drill chuck.

Faceplates

Most lathes come standard with a pair of centers (page 30) and one or more faceplates. Faceplates are useful for mounting non-spindle work—that is, any project that will be turned without needing the tailstock to support the workpiece. Examples of this are bowls, platters, and turned boxes.

Common sizes

There really is no standard in faceplate sizes. There are almost as many sizes as there are lathe manufacturers. However, the common sizes you'll find are 3", 4", 6", 8", and 10".

Quality faceplates with be cast and then machined flat. They'll also have a series of rings scribed into the front to make it easier to center blanks on the plate, as shown in the upper left photo. You'll also find at least two sets of holes for mounting screws to attach a blank. ShopTip: If you turn green wood, drive screws through as many holes as possible to better grip the wet wood; many pro turners actually drill extra holes for even more screw-holding power.

Faceplate rings

Unlike a faceplate that threads onto the headstock spindle, a faceplate ring (upper right photo) is gripped by the jaws of a scroll chuck (see the sidebar on page 65 for more on using faceplate rings). A faceplate ring is screwed onto the back of a workpiece, allowing it to be firmly gripped by most scroll chucks. Why use a faceplate ring in lieu of a faceplate? Turners who work green wood use these rings all the time. In fact, they often have stacks of them that they attach to green blanks for rough turning and leave in place until the work is ready for final turning. This ensures that the blank can be remounted easily, accurately, and securely.

DOUBLE-SIDED TAPE FOR FACEPLATE WORK

A common problem when using a faceplate is dealing with the holes that the mounting screws leave in the blank. One way to get around this problem is to not use screws in the first place. Instead, you can attach a blank to a faceplate with double-sided tape. Granted, this isn't as secure as screws, but with a good-quality tape, you can achieve a sound grip that's solid enough to handle many turning tasks. A couple of words of caution here. First, make sure to use a cloth-based tape. Most turning catalogs sell tape designed specifically for turners. Don't use the thin plastic stuff—it won't grip the workpiece securely. Second, in order to get the optimum grip, both the faceplate and the blank must be flat and smooth. Check both with a straightedge and flatten either as needed.

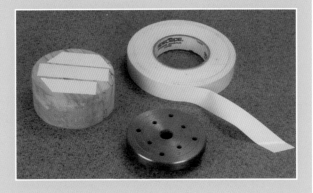

Turning Centers

Turning centers are short, tapered metal rods that fit into the spindles of the headstock and tailstock (see the drawing below). The headstock center is commonly referred to as a drive center and typically has two or four spurs (see the drawing below) that are driven into the workpiece to grip it. When the motor is turned on, the center will "drive" the wood, spinning it at the selected speed. Tailstock centers support the opposite end of a blank and allow it to spin freely. They either have a cup (dead) center or a live center, as shown in the drawing. Regardless of the center type, the taper, called a Morse taper, is usually one of two sizes: Morse taper #1 or #2.

Drive centers

Multi-prong centers are used to drive or spin a blank. They have two or four prongs, as shown in the top two photos. We prefer four-prong centers, as there's less of a tendency to split a workpiece. Whichever type you use, make sure to periodically sharpen the prongs with a small mill file so they can penetrate the wood easily to provide a secure grip.

Tailstock centers

Unlike a cup center in a tailstock where the workpiece rubs against the "rim" of the cup and will eventually burn (bottom right photo), a live center uses a ball-bearing cap or cone that spins along with the workpiece (right photo, second from bottom). Live centers have all but replaced cup centers these days and are generally shipped as standard with most lathes.

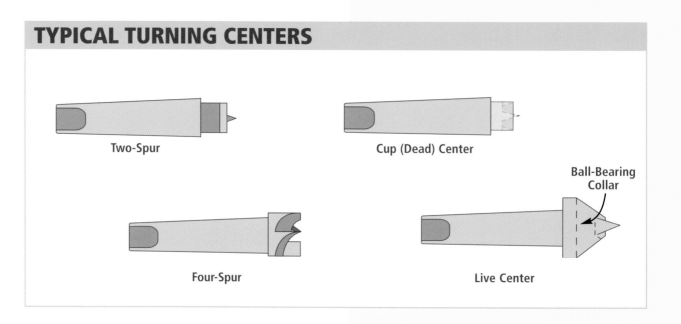

TYPICAL TURNING CENTERS

Two-Spur

Cup (Dead) Center

Four-Spur

Live Center

Ball-Bearing Collar

Tool Rests

The tool rest of a lathe allows you to present the lathe tool to the workpiece at the proper height and position. Since you'll use the tool rest for virtually every cut you make, it's important to know what makes a good one and what types are available. A quality tool rest will be made of cast iron and have smooth, flat milled surfaces that contact the bed. The adjustment knob on the rest base should be spring-loaded so you can pivot it out of the way once the rest is locked in place. There are three basic types of tool rests available: straight, bowl, and external.

Straight rests

Straight tool rests come in a variety of lengths and will be the rests you use most often (upper left photo). An 8" to 10" rest is commonly included with most lathes, and you can purchase shorter 6" rests and longer 24" rests from most manufacturers. Rests longer than 12" typically have double shafts (inset photo below) and will require an additional tool rest base for proper operation. Longer rests like this are worth their weight in gold when it comes to shaping long spindles. They allow you to make a continuous smooth cut instead of stopping frequently to reposition the rest.

Bowl rests

Specialized tool rests have been developed to help turners safely create bowls. They come in two flavors: S-shaped and right-angle (top right photo). Both work well to better support a lathe tool inside the bowl. Without this type of rest, the lathe tool would extend out precariously past the rest and would vibrate excessively and would most likely catch and cause a nasty accident.

External rests

An external rest is used for "outboard" turning—that is, turning that's not done over the lathe bed. Some lathes offer outboard capabilities by allowing you to attach a faceplate to the opposite end of the headstock or else the headstock pivots to bring the drive center in front of the lathe or at its side. Since the tool rest that slides along the bed is no longer functional, here's where an external rest comes in (photo at right). Many lathe manufacturers sell only the base because the head will accept their standard tool rests.

STEADY RESTS

A steady rest is a lathe accessory that slides along and clamps to the bed of the lathe (photo at left). It typically has three adjustable arms that are tipped with rollers to support long and/or thin workpieces. These are particularly useful when turning spindles for chairs, cribs, and other projects. Instead of buying one of these, you can make your own; see pages 106–109 for more on this.

Gouges

Although there are a wide variety of turning tools available, they can all be broadly classified into one of four groups: gouges, chisels, scrapers, and specialty tools. For the most part, a turning tool consists of a metal blade or rod that's shaped for a specific task that's fitted into a wood handle, usually via a tang with a ferrule to prevent the handle from splitting. Prices vary vastly, depending primarily on the quality and thickness of the tool steel. Quality lathe tools use premium high-speed steel (around Rockwell C60 to C62) with thick, stiff blades.

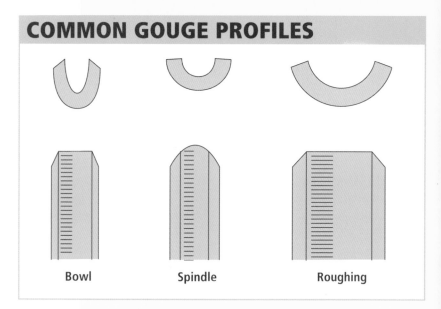

COMMON GOUGE PROFILES

Bowl   Spindle   Roughing

Roughing

A roughing gouge is a type of gouge that's designed for rough work—in particular, truing up a workpiece (taking it from square or octagonal to round). A roughing gouge can be identified by its square end (photo above and drawing above right). Leaving the end of the gouge square like this creates a sturdier edge, but limits the amount of close-in work you can do with it. A 1" roughing gouge is a good addition to any turning tool set.

Spindle

By far the most common type of gouge in use by avid turners is the spindle gouge (bottom photo). The tip of a spindle gouge is oval-shaped, and the flute is generally shallow (compared to a deep-flute or bowl gouge; see the opposite page). This type of profile is ideal for

general shaping and is especially adept at handling small details. The $1/2$" size is the most common, with turners often adding a $3/8$" and $1/4$" gouge to their turning set.

Fingernail

A fingernail, or finger tip, gouge is so named because its business end is shaped much like the tip of a finger (photo at right). The finger-shaped tip allows you to reach in and turn delicate details where other gouges can't go without catching. Fingernail gouges can be referred to as spindle gouges, but the profile or "wings" are generally deeper along the sides than on a spindle gouge, allowing for a "pull" or "shearing" cut that is becoming increasingly popular with turners. Fingernail gouges are commonly available in $1/4$", $3/8$", and $1/2$" sizes, with blade lengths averaging around 6".

Bowl

Bowl gouges are similar to spindle or fingertip gouges except they're usually made square ends and with stouter blades and longer handles (these tools are sometimes referred to as "long and strong" gouges; see below). Blade lengths vary from 8" to 18", and handles can be anywhere from 14" to 24" in length (top photo). Both of these create a tool that's less susceptible to vibration and can be safely extended a bit farther past a tool rest. The $1/2$" bowl gouge is the favorite size of most bowl turners.

Mastercut gouges

Mastercut gouges are manufactured by Oneway (www.oneway.on.ca) and are designed to fit into their Sure-Grip handles. These excellent tools are double-ended (middle photo) so that you can grind different bevels on the two ends—or the same bevel and save yourself a trip to the grinder or sharpening stone. Manufactured of superior steel, these gouges hold their edge longer than conventional gouges and are easier to sharpen. Various grinds provide gouges that can be used for delicate finishing work or taking heavy cuts while allowing maximum chip flow.

LONG AND STRONG LATHE TOOLS

Long and strong tools are a class of tools designed to handle challenging turning jobs where you need to extend the tool well past the tool rest. They can handle this, as either the blade or handle is longer—or both. At the same time, the blades are generally much thicker and the handles are stouter. This way when the blade is positioned past the tool rest, the tool will help dampen vibration. In the bottom photo, compare the long and strong gouge at the top of the photo with the standard gouge below it (we placed a drive center in the photo to give you an idea of the scale of these beefy tools).

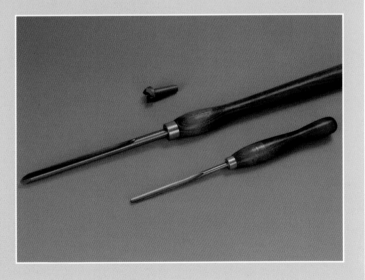

Chisels

Lathe chisels are primarily used for delicate and finishing cuts. They produce a smooth surface that's second to none. Common types include the skew chisel, flat chisel, and oval skew chisel (see the drawing below).

Skew

Of all the lathes tools out there, the skew chisel (top photo) has the worst reputation for being troublesome. And it is—when you first start turning. But with some practice, a skew chisel can be invaluable for smoothing cylinders, cutting in details, and a variety of other tasks. The reason chisels can be troublesome is that it's very easy to "catch" the workpiece with the sharp ends. When this occurs, the chisel end digs into the workpiece and tears the wood. Proper technique will usually prevent this (see pages 54–55 for more on this). Another way to "tame" the skew is to modify the grind; see page 55 for more on this. Chisels come either skewed or flat, in sizes ranging from $1/4$" in width up to $1^{1}/4$".

Oval skew

The primary difference between a skew chisel and an oval skew chisel can be seen by examining the cross

sections of the tool shanks, as shown in the drawing below. A skew chisel has a rectangular shank, and an oval skew has an oval or rounded shank (bottom right photo). What this does is allows the oval skew to travel more smoothly along a tool rest without catching, as the sharp edges of a standard skew chisel are prone to do. Note: You can soften the square edges of a standard skew chisel by grinding them away; see page 145 for more on this.

CHISEL PROFILES

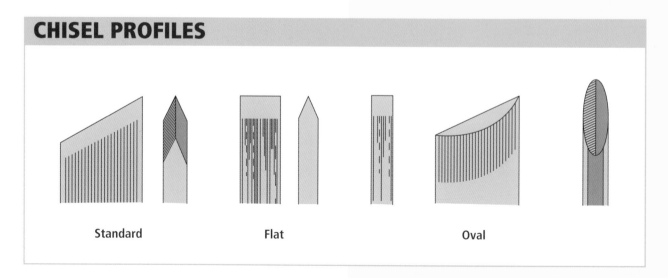

Standard	Flat	Oval

Scrapers

Scrapers are tools that cut wood with a scraping action instead of a pure cutting action that a gouge or chisel produces. They're typically made from flat stock, and the ends are beveled in the desired shape. If you treat a lathe scraper the same way you treat a hand scraper—that is, you burnish an edge on it—the lathe scraper is also capable of producing whisper-thin shavings. Although some woodturners look down on scrapers, these tools are easy to use and are commonly used by world-class production turners. You'll find two common profiles (square and round) and a multitude of specialty profiles, including dovetail profiles (see below) and various partially rounded profiles. Additionally, some tool makers now offer multi-tip scrapers (see the sidebar below).

Square-end

Square-end scrapers (photo at left) are ideal for flattening the bottoms of bowls, platters, and turned boxes. If sharpened and burnished properly (see pages 144 and 154, respectively), most scrapers can be used for moderate to intense shaping work. A finely tuned scraper is also one of the best ways to get a smooth finish on difficult-to-turn woods such as burls and other highly figured woods. Square-end scrapers come in widths ranging from $1/2$" all the way up to 2".

Round-end

The ends of round-nose scrapers (top photo) may be a perfect half-circle, an oval, or anything in between. Like their square-end cousins, they are useful for cleaning up tough-to-turn woods and work especially well for finishing up inside turned boxes. Sizes here also vary from $1/2$" in width up to 2".

Dovetail

The profile of a dovetail scraper is designed specifically to shape the inside lip of a recess intended to fit over the angled jaws of a scroll chuck (see page 26). If you do a lot of work with a scroll chuck, consider investing in one of these, as the profile of the tool will cut the perfect angle to mate with the jaws of your chuck—just make sure to purchase this tool from the same manufacturer that made your chuck, to ensure that the angles are compatible.

MULTI-TIP SCRAPERS

Quality lathe tools are expensive. One way to save money on a set of scrapers is to purchase a multi-tip scraper set. By using a common handle with interchangeable tips, you can save considerable money. The only disadvantage is the time and energy required to change tips. This can be frustrating if you frequently need to change from scraper to scraper during a project.

Specialty Tools

Any lathe tool that doesn't fit into one of the gouge, chisel, or scraper classifications is a specialty tool. These can be gouges or scrapers that are modified for a specific task, such as truing up the interior of a bowl or turned box. Specialty tools include chatter tools, micro tuning tools, ring tools, parting tools, hollowing tools, mushroom tools, and beaders.

Chatter tool

Chatter tools (top photo) are designed to create decorative textures on turned objects. The tool consists of an adjustable blade that's pointed on one end. The blade is intentionally thin so that when it comes in contact with the tool, it'll chatter and leave behind a decorative surface. In effect, the tip of the tool will chatter along the surface and cut out tiny chips. These tools are best used on the end grain of tightly grained woods (see page 98 for more on using this interesting tool).

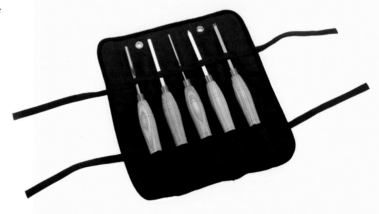

Micro turning tools

Micro turning tools are basically mini-sized turning tools. These diminutive tools typically come in sets (middle photo) and are often only 6" to 8" long from end to end. They are particularly useful for turning small, intricate, detailed work such as spindles for doll furniture, jewelry, and any other project that requires a fine touch. Because of their small size, they can also come to the rescue in tight quarters where a larger tool can't fit.

Ring tool

Ring tools (bottom photo) are specifically designed for end-grain hollowing. They often have a dual bevel—one on the larger-diameter side and one on the smaller-diameter side—to allow for hollowing of internal curved surfaces and flat-bottomed vessels. These tools produce remarkably smooth surfaces on tough-to-turn end grain. They are ideal for turning end-grain boxes, goblets, and egg cups and are typically available in 1/2" and 1" sizes.

Parting tool

Although the parting tool (top photo) is technically a scraper, it's usually sold as a specialty tool. Parting tools are used to "part off" or remove, or prepare to remove, a workpiece from the lathe. They are also commonly used in conjunction with a caliper (page 24) to define diameters on a workpiece. That is, after you've marked the profile of a workpiece, you use the parting tool to cut down to the desired diameter, using the caliper to identify when you've removed sufficient stock.

Deep hollowing tool

Deep hollowing tools are specialized versions of ring tools. They are designed for hollowing deep forms and vessels. Most hollowing tools (middle photo) have a top section that is adjustable to give you complete control over the depth of cut. Deep hollowing tools are available either straight or swan-necked. The swan-necked design is used to cut away near the rim of the vessel, while the standard tool is for the bottom of a vessel.

Mushroom tool

The mushroom tool (bottom photo) was created by Roger Warren and is designed with the beginner in mind. It is used to create the underneath portion of a mushroom where the hood connects to the stem. Although this may seem of limited use, the finely curved tip lends itself well to turning fine details where other tools can't reach.

Beaders

Beaders or beading tools are basically specialty scrapers designed to cut a specific-sized bead. With a little practice, however, you can use one of these to cut a wide variety of bead diameters, as shown in the top photo. The end of the beader comes to a fine point to define the valley between the beads. A curved profile on each side of the point creates one-half of the rounded bead profile. By varying the position of the tool, you can cut various-sized beads.

CORING SYSTEMS

Technically not a tool, but more of an accessory, a coring system like the Oneway Easy-Core system shown here is a great way to save wood (www.oneway.on.ca). When most turners want to turn a bowl, they spend considerable time and energy hollowing out the inside of the bowl. The sad thing about this technique is that all that good wood inside the bowl ends up as shavings. Enter a coring system, to the rescue. These systems are designed to literally scoop out the inside in one piece so that you can use this to turn one or more additional bowls.

The heart of these systems is a cutter and tool rest with matching curves. Both of these fit into a heavy-duty base that clamps securely to your lathe bed. After some simple setup, you pivot the cutter into the spinning blank and it cores out the inside. The Oneway system shown here comes in three base unit sizes (16", 20", and 24") and has four different knife sets (9"-diameter, 11½"-diameter, 13¼"-diameter, and 16¼"-diameter). Any size lathe with a 16" to 26" swing and a flat bed can accomodate this system. (For more on using a coring system, see pages 86–89.)

Sanding and Buffing

Sanding on a lathe can be a challenge because when sandpaper comes in contact with the rotating workpiece, it tends to leave swirl marks. One way to get around this is to sand with a pad or disk fitted in an electric drill. Because the rotations of the lathe and the drill are offset, you get a sanding action that's somewhat similar to that of a random-orbit sander.

Snap or twist systems

A popular sanding system among production turners is a snap- or twist-together disk system like the one shown in the upper left photo. These systems generally consist of a disk holder that fits into your

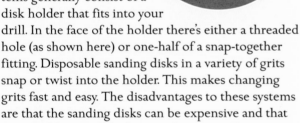

drill. In the face of the holder there's either a threaded hole (as shown here) or one-half of a snap-together fitting. Disposable sanding disks in a variety of grits snap or twist into the holder. This makes changing grits fast and easy. The disadvantages to these systems are that the sanding disks can be expensive and that most holders are flat plastic and not very forgiving.

Sanding pads

A more forgiving type of sandpaper holder is the pads shown in the top right photo that insert a foam cushion between the hard plastic shank holder and the sandpaper. Some systems offer even more padding by supplied hook-and-loop pads that attach to the primary foam pad. The surfaces of both the primary sanding pad and additional pads accept hook-and-loop sandpaper.

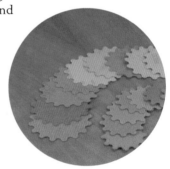

Specialty paper

There's a nifty new line of sanding disks designed with turners in mind (middle right photo). New Abrasives (www.newabrasives.com) manufactures New Wave sanding disks with a unique perimeter profile. This unique profile helps prevent slices caused by the edge of ordinary sanding disks. Grit sizes are available from 60 up to an astonishing 14,000. Although disk sizes range from 2" up to 11", turners will find the 2" and 3" sizes the most appropriate. New Abrasives also sells bowl-sanding kits that include one hook-and-loop sanding pad (with a 1/4" shank), one hard and one soft inner face pad, and five each of 60-, 120-, 220-, and 320-grit sanding pads.

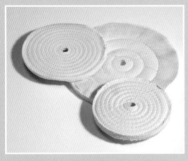

Buffing pads. A wide variety of different shapes and sizes of buffing pads are available to fit your lathe, grinder, drill, or drill press.

Polishing compounds. Bare buffing pads do a decent job of buffing, but if you're after a polishing action, you'll want to "load" you pads with a polishing compound. The four most common types are, from right to left: emery (black), Tripoli (brown), white, and red rouge.

BUFFING ACCESSORIES

Many turners like to polish their projects to a glossy finish. One way to achieve this high-gloss finish is by buffing.

3 Basic Lathe Techniques

A lathe in the shop will open up a new world of projects that you can tackle. Always wanted to make a Boston rocker? How about a pie-crust table or a set of wooden dishes? All of these projects and a lot more are viable with a lathe in the shop. Granted, most of these are challenging and you'll want to start with simpler projects using basic lathe techniques.

And that's what this chapter is all about—mastering the basic techniques of turning before moving on to challenging techniques such as bowl turning (see Chapter 4 for more on this). Fundamental techniques for the lathe in this chapter include preparing and mounting stock, truing and shaping blanks, basic shaping, sanding, and finishing.

All of these techniques and more are covered in detail here so that you can confidently flip on your lathe and get started spewing shavings around the shop.

Parting off is one of the many basic techniques described in this chapter that will get you turning projects from start to finish on the lathe in no time.

Lathe Safety

Lathes are inherently safe machines. They are the only stationary power tool with which you present the cutting tool to the workpiece instead of the workpiece to the cutting tool, as is the case with a table saw, band saw, and jointer. It might surprise you, then, to see the long list of safety rules on the opposite page. Just because the lathe is a basically safe machine doesn't mean you can't hurt yourself. Most of these rules are common sense, but it doesn't hurt to reiterate each one. Regardless of the project you're turning and the techniques you'll be using, it's important to start by protecting yourself: Wear proper clothes and protect your eyes, ears, and lungs.

of goggles (top right photo). Don't wear safety glasses unless they have side protectors—quite often this is where debris gets in. Some lathe motors whine significantly, and you should also don earplugs or muffs to prevent long-term hearing loss.

Wear proper attire

No, we're not talking about a black tie. Proper turning attire means no long sleeves. If your shirt does have long sleeves, roll the sleeves up to about your elbow, as shown in the middle left photo. Better yet, put on a short-sleeved shirt, as all the rolled cuffs will do is capture dust and chips that you'll end up distributing in the bedroom when you change clothes. Tuck in shirttails, remove dangling jewelry, and tie back long hair. Many turners prefer a turner's smock or a turtleneck-style shirt, as these prevent dust and chips from snaking down inside your shirt (rather annoying, actually).

Protect your eyes and ears

Dust and shavings can peel off a workpiece at astonishing speeds. Keep this debris out of your eyes by wearing a face shield (bottom left photo) or a pair

Protect your lungs

The U.S. Environmental Protection Agency has classified wood dust as a carcinogen. Keep harmful dust out of your lungs with a mask, a respirator, or better yet, an air-filtration helmet like the one shown in the bottom right photo. This helmet is made by RACAL (a division of 3M) and it pulls air in through a filter/battery pack that fits onto a belt around your waste. Purified air is then pumped up though the flexible hose connecting the pack to the helmet and gently flows over the face. This not only provides cool, clean air, but it also prevents the face shield from fogging up.

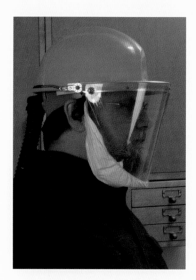

WOODTURNING SAFETY GUIDELINES

1 **Know the tool.** Read and follow all warning labels and manufacturer's owner's/operator's manual before using a lathe, lathe tool, or accessory.

2 **Protect your eyes.** Shavings and dust can be hurled off a turned object at surprising speed. Wear a face shield or goggles whenever the lathe is turned on.

3 **Protect your lungs.** Wood dust is harmful to your lungs. Wear a dust mask, respirator, or air-filtration helmet when turning and use any dust collection available.

4 **Protect your ears.** Make sure to wear ear plugs or ear muffs to keep out harmful noise when turning, to reduce the risk of long-term hearing loss.

5 **Wear safe clothing.** Loose clothing, long sleeves, and jewelry that can dangle all pose safety risks, as they can become entangled in the lathe. Roll up sleeves, tuck in shirts, and remove jewelry before operating a lathe. If you have long hair, tie it back to keep it out of the lathe.

6 **Don't speed.** Consult your lathe owner's manual for matching the correct speed to the task at hand. In general, use slower speeds for large-diameter and heavy workpieces. Also, use slower speeds for roughing cuts and higher speeds for finish cuts.

7 **Check and double-check.** Never start a lathe before checking to make sure the workpiece will safely clear the tool rest and bed of the lathe. Rotate the workpiece by hand and when satisfied, double-check that all clamps and levers are tight and out of the way.

8 **Mount up.** Before energizing the lathe, make sure the workpiece is securely mounted in the lathe; check the headstock, tailstock, and any chucks in use to make sure they're adjusted properly.

9 **Keep it close.** Keep the tool rest as close as possible to the workpiece at all times. This reduces the amount of tool that extends unsupported past the tool rest.

10 **Guards in place.** Double-check that all safety guards, including belt and motor guards, are securely in place before turning on the lathe.

11 **Rest easy.** Be sure to place a tool on the tool rest before beginning a cut to prevent the workpiece from slamming the tool down onto the rest at the beginning of the cut.

12 **Know thyself.** Some techniques are best left for more experienced turners. Know your limitations and practice new techniques on small pieces, taking it slow as you go.

13 **The tailstock is your friend.** Whenever possible, use the tailstock to provide extra support. This added insurance can prevent a nasty accident from happening (such as a workpiece flying off the lathe).

14 **Sand alone.** Always remove the tool rest before sanding. One of the most common lathe accidents is getting one's fingers caught between the workpiece and the tool rest when sanding—get it out of there.

15 **Don't reach out.** Although many turning tools have thick, stout blades, it's never safe to extend a tool well past the tool rest. In cases like these, consider using a curved or angled tool rest to provide better support to the tool.

16 **Stay sharp.** Keep your tools ground at the proper angles and honed sharp. A dull tool is always more dangerous than a sharp one, and the operator tends to force the cut. New tools should be sharpened before first use, as these tend to be ground to the correct profile, but not honed.

17 **Don't go there.** Use tools, chucks, and accessories only for their intended purpose; to do otherwise is asking for an accident.

18 **Check it out.** Inspect your lathe frequently to make sure all is in working order. Keep the bed, tool rest, headstock, and tailstock clean, free from rust, and sealed against moisture.

19 **Don't walk away.** Never leave your lathe running unattended. To prevent accidents, make sure you turn it off when it's not in use.

20 **Relax.** One of the keys to safe, successful turning is to develop a comfortable, well-balanced stance. Likewise, keep a firm but gentle grip on the tool; a white-knuckle grip will not give you more control—it will cause muscle fatigue that can easily lead to an accident.

21 **Don't crack up.** Use caution and common sense when turning stock that has cracks, splits, checks, knots, or bark. Face protection is essential here, as chunks of the workpiece could come flying off at any time.

Preparing for Spindle Work

Before you can mount a workpiece in the lathe, it must be prepared: Centerpoints need to be defined on the ends of spindles, and a kerf should be cut for the drive center.

Mark diagonals

There are a number of ways you can quickly find the center of a workpiece. The combination square is the perfect tool for the job. To locate dead center, use the 45-degree head of the square to mark a series of diagonals (top left photo). This works best with stock that is relatively square, since sides that are not 90-degree can throw the centerpoint off. Alternatively, place the edge of a straightedge so it is centered on opposite diagonals and mark a line; do this for the opposite set of diagonals; where the lines cross is the center of the blank.

Using a center finder

Finding the center of a workpiece is a common layout task. It's so common that a number of tool manufacturers make center finders like the one shown in the bottom left photo specifically for this task. These simple tools have lips on two adjacent sides to quickly position the workpiece so you can mark dead center. To use a center finder, press the edges of the workpiece up against the lips of the center finder. Then butt a pencil or marking knife against the center cutout and draw along this to mark a line. Next, rotate the workpiece 90 degrees and make another mark. Where the lines intersect is dead center.

Punch and drill

Once you've located the center on each end of the blank, use a centerpunch to make a depression in the center for starting a drill bit, as shown in the bottom right photo. Then drill shallow holes in each end at the centerpoint (inset photo): one for the main spur of the drive center and one for the center of the tailstock center. We typically use an 1/8" bit and drill a 3/16" or so deep hole. These holes just make it a lot easier to chuck the blank accurately between centers. And holes like this are particularly useful when working with hardwoods, especially dense species like ebony, cocobolo, or rosewood.

PARALLEL-LINE TECHNIQUE

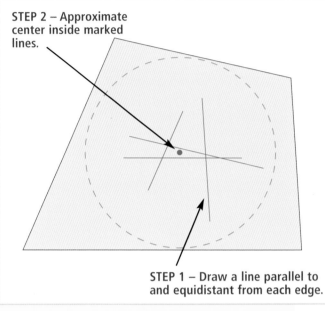

STEP 2 – Approximate center inside marked lines.

STEP 1 – Draw a line parallel to and equidistant from each edge.

Marking odd-shaped pieces

Depending on the stock you choose to turn, you may occasionally (or frequently) find the need to chuck up a blank that's not square. All of the prior methods don't work for an out-of-square blank. So how do you find it? Try the parallel-line technique illustrated in the top drawing. It won't find the perfect center, but it will get you close enough for turning.

Cutting kerfs by hand

The spurs on drive centers will stay sharper longer if you first make one or two diagonal kerfs in the end of the workpiece (middle photo). This also makes it a lot easier to center the drive spur. Take a pass or two with a small backsaw, gent's saw, or dovetail saw, and continue until the kerfs are about 1/8" deep.

Cutting kerfs with a band saw

If you've got a lot of turning to do—say for example you're going to turn spindles for a set of dining chairs—you can save yourself considerable time and effort by cutting kerfs on all the blanks with a band saw as shown in the bottom photo. Simply tilt the table of the saw to 45 degrees and bring the rip fence close to the blade without it touching. Now turn on the saw and gently press the end of each spindle blank against the spinning blade. Then pull the blank back, rotate it 90 degrees, and make another cut to create perfect diagonal crosshairs for your drive center. Additionally, if the blank is large, consider knocking off the corners to reduce the waste you'll have to remove when truing up the cylinder; see the sidebar on page 47 for more on this.

Mounting a Spindle Blank

Once you've prepared a blank for spindle work—or turning between centers—the next step is to mount the blank on the lathe.

Position the drive center in the blank

Since the bulk of spindle work is done using the drive center to rotate the stock, the first thing to is to position the drive center on the blank. If you've prepared the blank as described on pages 44–45, this is easy to do. If the blank is hardwood, it's often best to drive the center into the end of the blank with a hammer, as shown in the top left photo. Align the prongs on the drive center with the kerfs in the end of the blank, and tap the drive center a few times with a hammer. For softer woods, this may not be necessary, as the pressure exerted by the tailstock is generally sufficient to get the prongs of the drive center to engage in the kerfs in the blank.

Position the blank in the headstock

Now you can insert the drive center into the head-stock spindle as shown in the upper right photo. Simply slide the Morse taper into its matching taper in the headstock and push the blank and center firmly in place. Do not drive the blank or the drive center in with a hammer at this point or you can lodge the Morse taper in the headstock so firmly that it will be difficult to remove later. For softwoods, it's often possible to slip the Morse taper in place first, then align the kerfs in the blank with the drive center

prongs and hold this in position while you slide the tailstock over to support the other end of the blank (see below).

Slide the tailstock over

The other end of the spindle blank is supported by the tailstock center. Before positioning the tailstock, it's a good idea to back the tailstock center as far back into the tailstock as possible—this will give you the maximum possible extension once the tailstock is in place. This also minimizes how far the tailstock center extends past the tailstock; the farther out it extends, the less rigid it will be. And you want the tailstock to be as rigid as possible to reduce vibration. Release the tailstock clamp and slide the tailstock over until the tip of the tailstock center engages the hole you drilled in the end of the blank. Then lock the tailstock firmly in place with the tailstock clamp.

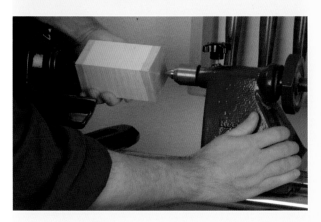

Add oil for dead centers

Most lathes these days are shipped with "live" or ball-bearing centers, where the tip of the center rides on ball or roller bearings and spins along with the blank. You may come across a "dead" center, where the tip is fixed in place. In cases like this, the blank will rotate on the tip of the center. Dead centers and cup centers will benefit from some lubrication to reduce friction and overheating, which can scorch the wood. A drop or two of light machine oil applied to the tip of the center as shown in the middle photo will do the job.

Adjust the tailstock pressure

The spindle blank needs to be held firmly in place between the headstock and tailstock. You can apply pressure to the blank by first releasing the tailstock center clamp and then adjusting the position of the tailstock center. The closer it's positioned to the head-stock, the greater the pressure. Increase tension as needed by rotating the tailstock center hand wheel as shown in the top photo. Don't go overboard here—all you need is for the prongs of the drive center to seat firmly in the kerfs you cut in the blank and for there to be no play in the spindle. Once you've applied sufficient pressure, secure the tailstock center clamp.

KNOCKING OFF CORNERS ON LARGE BLANKS

If the spindle blank you intend to turn is large, it's a good idea to first knock the corners off, either on a table saw or on a band saw as shown here. Eliminating the corners and converting the blank to an octagon does a couple things. First, is reduces the weight of the blank and therefore reduces vibration. Second, it removes a lot of waste that you'd normally have to remove with a roughing gouge. Not only does this save time, but it also lessens wear and tear on your tools. To remove the corners on a band saw, tilt the table to 45 degrees, then position the band saw fence to remove the desired amount. Remove one corner, rotate 90 degrees, and cut. Repeat for the remaining corners.

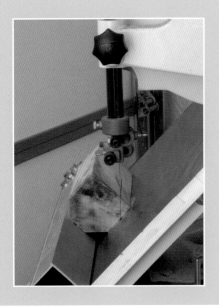

Positioning the Tool Rest

The catch phrase you'll hear over and over again from turning instructors is "make sure the bevel is rubbing." That's the secret to using most cutting tools. What it means is you should position the tool so it's supported by the tool rest and so the bevel of the tool is riding on the workpiece. The simplest way to do this is to start with the tool so the is handle pointing down. Place the bevel against the workpiece and simply raise the handle until cutting begins. As long as you keep the shank or blade of the tool against the tool rest and bevel on the workpiece, cutting should be smooth and sweet. This goes for both gouges and chisels, too.

Slide tool rest in place

The first step to positioning the tool rest is to get it roughly in place. Release the tool rest base clamp and slide it up to the blank as close as possible without making contact, as shown in the top photo. Then rotate the blank by hand to make sure it clears the tool rest. Readjust as needed and then lock down the tool rest base clamp.

Tool rest height for spindle work

There is—and always will be—debate on the proper position for a tool rest. The correct placement for you will depend on the height of your lathe, your height, the tool you're using, and your working stance. If you're new to turning, start with the tool rest roughly centered on the blank as shown in the middle photo. Now lock the height in place with the tool rest clamp and make a test cut. Turn off the lathe and shift the rest up or down as needed to achieve a smooth cut. Many turners prefer the rest slightly above or below center—usually 1/8" either way, as shown in the drawing. Whichever tool rest position you're the most comfortable with is the correct height for you. Note: Tool rest placement for scrapers differs substantially from gouge and chisel work; see pages 52–53 for more on this.

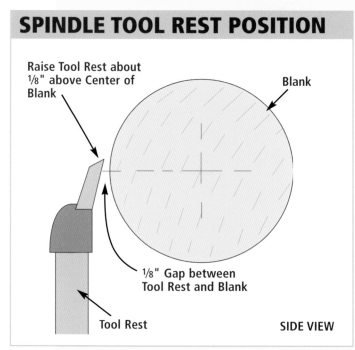

SPINDLE TOOL REST POSITION

Raise Tool Rest about 1/8" above Center of Blank

Blank

1/8" Gap between Tool Rest and Blank

Tool Rest

SIDE VIEW

FACEPLATE TOOL REST POSITION

Position Tool Rest 1/8" below Center of Blank

Faceplate-Mounted Blank

1/8" Gap between Tool Rest and Blank

Tool Rest

SIDE VIEW

Tool rest height for faceplate work

Unlike spindle work, faceplate work has two different tool rest positions: one for working on the rim of the blank, and one for turning the face of the blank. As with spindle work, you'll want the tool rest as close as possible to the blank without making contact, as shown in the middle photo. When working on the rim, your tool rest position will vary widely due to the tool you're using. As we've mentioned, the idea is to get the bevel to rub on the blank as well as resting on the tool rest.

With different-diameter blanks, this can mean positioning the tool rest slightly above or below the centerline as shown in the top left drawing. Tool rest position for working on the face will also hover around the centerline. To turn right to the center of the blank with a wide gouge, the tool rest will need to be slightly below the centerline. Here again, this will take some trial and error for you to determine the best height for you.

When turning long stock

Tool rest position for long stock is identical to that for shorter stock, with the exception that you'll need to constantly move and reposition the tool rest along the length of the blank, as shown in the bottom photo. This is where a long tool rest with double shafts will really pay off, as the need for repositioning is eliminated (see page 31). If you have only a short tool rest, make sure to turn off the lathe and allow the blank to come to a complete stop before repositioning the tool rest. A lot of really nice spindle work has been ruined over the years by turners who move the rest with the lathe turned on, only to have one end of the tool rest contact the spinning wood, damaging the piece.

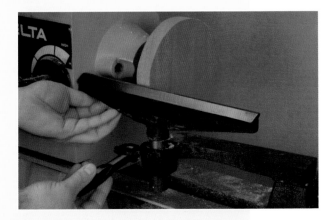

Turning a Rough Cylinder

One of the most basic turning techniques is turning a blank into a rough cylinder. This is done so that you can lay out the profile on the blank and begin defining these points with a parting tool and caliper. Once these points are defined, you can shape the piece with a variety of tools.

Roughing-gouge position

The best tool for roughing out a cylinder is the roughing gouge. That's because its square-cut end and thick shank hold up well under the shock of encountering flats on the blank. If the stock you've chucked in the lathe is square, select a low speed and present the roughing gouge to the workpiece gently, but with a firm grip. Most turners tend to skew the gouge at a slight angle as they move it along the tool rest, as shown in the top photo. This does two things: It helps prevent the sharp corners of the tool from digging into the work, and also creates a cleaner, shearing cut.

Start in the center

As soon as you turn on the lathe with a square blank between the centers, you'll notice a "ghost" profile of the blank caused by the gaps between the corners of the blank as it rotates. This ghost edge is what the roughing gouge needs to come in contact with as you turn. You'll want to take very light cuts at first, starting in the center and working out toward an end, as shown in the middle photo. As you continue to knock off the corners, this ghost profile will move closer and closer to the center of the blank until the blank is round and the ghost profile no longer exists.

Work toward ends

As you begin knocking off the corners of the blank, switch direction and work toward the other end. Stop the lathe periodically to check your progress and to

move the tool rest closer to the blank. As the blank gets closer and closer to being round, you can take deeper cuts (as shown in the bottom photo), and you'll notice the sound of the cutting action changing as the tool encounters smaller flats on the blank. Experienced turners can both hear and feel when a blank is round.

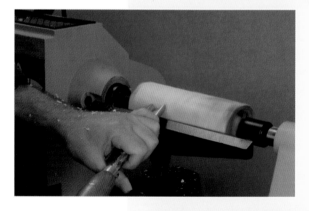

Make a full-length cut

Once the bulk of the corners are knocked off, stop the lathe and again move the tool rest closer to the workpiece. Then take a couple of full-length passes, moving the gouge along the full length of the blank to create a round cylinder, as shown in the top photo. Continue like this until you've turned a cylinder of the desired rough diameter; see below for a quick way to check the cylinder for roundness.

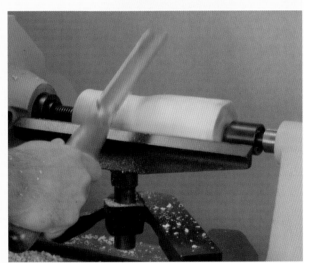

Chatter test

Here's a lathe trick that's been around almost as long as lathes. It was developed by production turners who didn't want to shut off their lathes just to check if their workpieces were round. What they did instead was leave the lathe on and place their turning tool gently on top of the spinning workpiece (middle photo). If the workpiece was round, the tool was still. If it wasn't, the tool bounced up and down—the higher it bounced, the more work they had left. There's also a telltale clicking or chatter noise every time the tool encounters a flat surface.

Skew chisel for smoother cut

If the cylinder you're turning needs to be round and finished smooth, consider using a skew chisel to smooth out the surface, as shown in the bottom photo. As you can see from the photo, thin, delicate shavings are produced with a skew chisel that will leave an unparalleled smooth surface. For more on using a skew chisel, see pages 54–55.

Scraping

Scrapers, if sharpened correctly and used properly, can leave a finish that rivals that of a sharp gouge or skew chisel. For a scraper to leave a finish this smooth, it must be prepared like a hand scraper. The business end must be ground and then honed smooth so a fine burr can be rolled on the end. Granted, you can scrape without a burr—but you'll tear out the wood fibers, leaving a rough surface instead of shearing them off. (For more on sharpening and burnishing scrapers, see pages 144 and 154, respectively.)

Tilt the scraper down

Scrapers are easy to use, and the only rule you need to follow religiously is to angle the end of the scraper down toward the lathe bed (middle photo). If you angle it up, a nasty catch can result. As always, keep the tool rest as close to the workpiece as possible while still allowing room for the lathe tool. When scraping a spindle, you'll generally want to raise the tool rest higher than you normally would so that when you tilt the scraper down it contacts the workpiece near its center, as illustrated in the top right drawing.

Slicing versus scraping

The controversy over scraping versus slicing or cutting will continue as long as there are more than two turners in the world. It's really a matter of personal preference; in our opinion there is no right or wrong answer. Much of the controversy results from improper scraping technique and poorly prepared scrapers. Notice the difference between the large clean shaving in the rear of the bottom photo, produced by a sharp scraper, and the small, almost dust-like shaving in the foreground, cut with a dull scraper. It's true that a cutting tool such as a skew chisel or gouge will produce a much smoother surface than one made with a poorly used or prepared scraper. But you can get similar results with a sharp scraper taking light cuts.

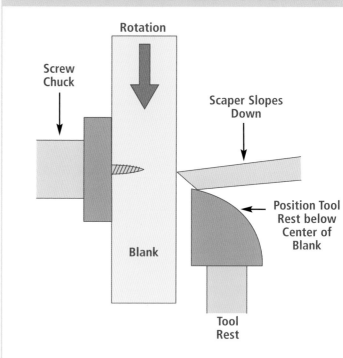

SCRAPING TOOL REST POSITION

Rotation

Screw Chuck

Scaper Slopes Down

Position Tool Rest below Center of Blank

Blank

Tool Rest

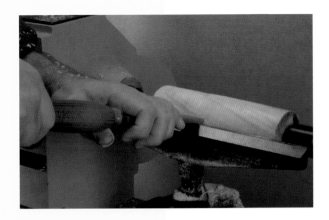

Proper hand position

Since there's much less of a chance of a scraper causing a catch—that is, where the tool inadvertently digs into the wood, causing damage—your hand position and grip can be fairly relaxed. What you want is a firm, light grip—no white knuckles. A typical comfortable position is one hand on the handle and one hand on the shank up near the tip, as shown in the top photo. The elbow of the arm that's holding the handle should be tucked into the body to create a stable base for the cut. If you let the hand at the tip rotate down far enough to contact the tool rest, you can use it sort of like an edge guide as you push the scraper along the blank to make a smooth, uniform pass.

Flat-nose scrapers

Flat-nose scrapers are ideal for flattening bottoms of bowls, trays, and platters. Unfortunately, they can be the most challenging scrapers to use, as the sharp corners can easily dig into the blank if the flat end of the scraper is not held perfectly parallel to the blank. One way around this is to knock off just the very tips of the scraper with a file or grinder to keep it from catching (see page 145 for more on this).

Round-nose scrapers

Round-nose scrapers are easy to use, as the rounded profile limits the potential for catches. When used aggressively, they can remove large amounts of stock in a hurry, as shown in the bottom photo. The only problem with this is that heavy cuts generally result in a rough surface. If you're after a smooth surface, burnish a fresh burr on the edge (see page 154) and take very light cuts.

Using a Skew Chisel

As we mentioned previously, the skew chisel is notorious for catching and digging into a workpiece. Besides proper technique (see below) there are a couple other things you can do to tame this wild beast. First, we recommend filing a slight round-over on the bottom edges of the tool along its length. This helps the tool slide more easily along the tool rest so it can't catch or bump in it, which can cause the tip to catch the workpiece (see page 145). Second, consider regrinding the profile of your chisel to form a gentle curve along the edge; see the sidebar on the opposite page.

Rotation

Direction of Cut

Blank

Cutting Portion of Skew Chisel

Tool position

One of the most difficult things to learn about using a skew chisel is to use a light grip. A death grip on this tool will only make your movements jerky, resulting in catches. Present the tool to the workpiece at an angle so neither the top nor bottom corner of the tip is contacting the workpiece (middle photo). This limits the actual cutting area to about one-half to one-third of its edge, as shown in the drawing. That's why the wider the chisel, the easier it is to use. We recommend that beginners practice with the widest chisel they've got.

Watch those corners

Move the chisel slowly along the tool rest, with your attention focused on the corners of the tool. A second's inattention can cause a nasty catch like the one shown in the bottom photo. It's surprising how little movement is required to cause a catch. That's why it's so important to use only a small portion of the cutting edge of the skew, maintain a steady grip, and keep your eyes on the corners.

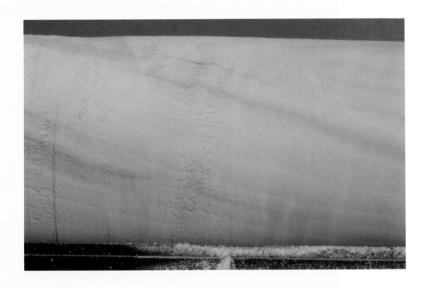

Surface quality

You'll find that once you start a cut with the bevel rubbing on the workpiece, the chisel will almost feed itself into the workpiece as it moves along. Take the time to sharpen a skew chisel as you would a plane blade (see page 152), and it will produce incredibly smooth cuts—look at the difference between the rough left-hand surface left by a gouge, and the silky-smooth surface on the right that was left by a skew chisel. Also, it's a shame that most turners use a skew chisel only for smoothing cylinders and gentle curves. It's also useful for fine detail work, such as cutting clean V-grooves, beads, and chamfers. When used with its point down, it cuts a cleaner shoulder than a parting tool (see page 63) because it slices instead of scrapes.

TAMING THE SKEW

MODIFIED SKEW CHISEL

Modified
Profile

Original
Profile

Reduce the possibility of a catch when using a skew chisel by modifying its profile as shown in the drawing at left. This can be done with a shop grinder, as long as long as you use a fine-grit wheel and quench the tool frequently to prevent it from losing its temper. Start by drawing the desired profile on the skew with a permanent marker, and then grind away the excess. Once you've achieved the desired profile, hone the edge with an oilstone.

Modified-profile skew chisels have become so popular that many of the tool manufacturers now offer the modified skew as one of their standard tools, like the one shown in the bottom photo made by Crown Tools. Additionally, most tool makers also offer oval skews, where the tool shank is oval versus rectangular to make it easier to move the tool along the rest without catching on the rest.

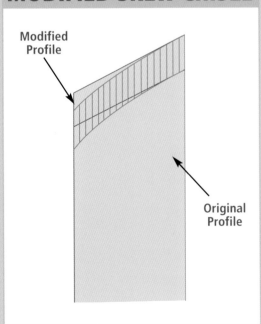

Marking Profiles

Unless you're turning freeform shapes on the lathe, you'll likely be following some kind of pattern. This means you'll want to mark the blank as needed to achieve the desired profile.

Pencil on tool rest

The most common way to mark a blank for turning a profile is to use a pencil laid on the tool rest as shown in the top photo. Typically, you'll measure to a specific spot with a ruler and then make a dark mark on the blank at the desired location with the pencil. When the lathe is then turned on, the mark will be slightly visible as it spins around. By pressing the pencil into the blank at the spinning mark, you can quickly draw a line around the entire blank. Make sure to rest the pencil on the tool rest for this, as an unsupported pencil can easily follow a rough surface and you'll end up with a crooked line or lines.

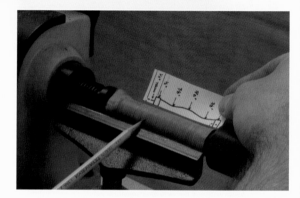

Half profile

Another common method for defining a profile on a blank is to use the pattern itself or a half profile like the one shown in the middle photo. Simply butt the half profile up against the blank and use a pencil to make marks at each specified location. Then remove the template, turn on the lathe, and use your pencil to convert the marks into lines as described above.

DUPLICATE WORK JIG

If you're faced with turning a set of identical parts, consider making a simple marking jig like the one shown in the photo at right. The jig is nothing more than a scrap of wood that you've glued on a half profile. Drill holes in the edge of the scrap at the desired marking locations, and drive in either brads (snip off their heads first) or thick pencil lead into the holes. Make sure they all protrude the same amount. To use the jig, just press it up against the spinning stock as shown to mark the profile. The advantage of using brads is they'll scribe the marks into the blank and won't dull like pencil lead.

Defining Cuts

After you've marked a profile on a blank, the next step is to define the profile further by cutting a kerf or groove at each location to the correct depth to match the desired diameter. The most common way to do this is with a parting tool and calipers as described below.

With a parting tool

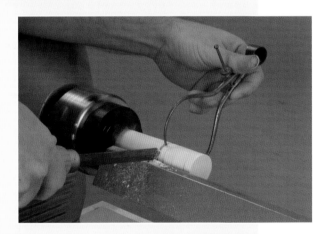

If you've got a good eye, you can define cuts by simply cutting a kerf with a parting tool as shown in the top photo. Some seasoned turners do this, but it requires a lot of practice to hit a diameter right on without a caliper. This technique is useful if you're experimenting with shapes or are creating a one-of-a-kind piece.

With a parting tool and calipers

More commonly, the parting tool is used with a pair of calipers set to the desired diameter. Since a parting tool is basically a scraper, you'll want to angle it slightly down as you cut, as shown in the middle photo. With a little practice, you'll find it easy to press the parting tool into the cut as you check its progress with calipers held in your other hand as shown. Allow the caliper tips to just barely touch the surface of the kerf as you cut. When you reach the desired diameter, the caliper ends will slip over the blank. We generally set the calipers to fit a tiny bit wider than needed to allow for final shaping and sanding.

Diamond-point scraper

It's not always necessary to use a parting tool to define a cut. A diamond-point scraper like the one shown in the bottom photo can also be used—but only for shallow cuts or to create a starting point for a chisel or gouge. Starting points are particularly useful when cutting near the edge of workpiece, to prevent a gouge or chisel from skipping out of position as it makes contact with the spinning workpiece (see page 70 for an example of this).

Turning a Cove

Coves are a nice decorative detail that can add visual interest to any project. They're surprisingly easy to turn, and with a little practice, you'll be making coves by the dozen.

Lay out the cove

The first step to turning a cove is to lay out its exact position and width. Even if you're practicing, this is a good idea, as most coves you turn will be part of a pattern such as a spindle leg. Turn off the lathe and locate the start and stop points of the cove. We often make a full-sized template from 1/4" hardboard to make duplicating parts easier—this also is a quick way to pick up diameters with a set of calipers. Just open them to fit over the template and they're set. Turn on the lathe and you'll see a ghosted line from the marks you made. Darken these with a pencil as shown in the top photo.

Cut one-half with a gouge

Many novice turners think that all you have to do to cut a cove is to shove a fingertip gouge into the wood and it'll cut a perfect cove. Well, it will cut a cove, but it will also severely tear the edges of the cove. The proper way to turn a cove is with a series of twisting cuts as illustrated in the drawing at right. You want to start with the gouge held almost vertical, as shown in the bottom photo. Then present the tool to the workpiece and press in and roll the gouge so that it ends up nearly horizontal—it's really a quick twist of the wrist—and one-half of the cove is done.

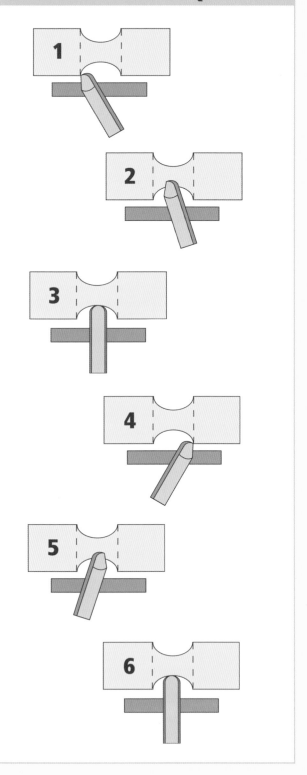

COVE-CUTTING SEQUENCE

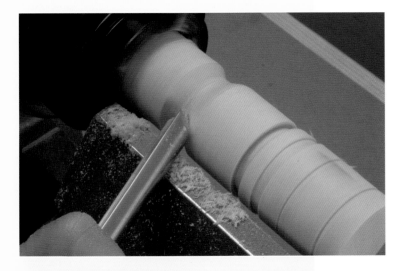

Cut the other half with a gouge

To finish the cove, start as you did for the first half except on the other side, as shown in the top photo. Here again, press in and twist to make the cut. With a little practice you can make a cove with two opposing cuts. If the two halves don't meet, pare away additional stock from the heavy side using the same technique.

Scraping a cove

You can also use a round-nose scraper to cut a cove, as shown in the middle photo. If you use a very sharp scraper and take light cuts, you can get a cove almost as clean as one cut with a gouge, with the exception of some modest tear-out at the edges of the cove. The technique is somewhat similar to using a gouge, except that the tool is kept flat on the tool rest and pointed down slightly. Start at one limit of the cove and pivot the scraper toward the center; then reverse direction and cut in from the other side. Remove stock in the center as needed to achieve the desired depth.

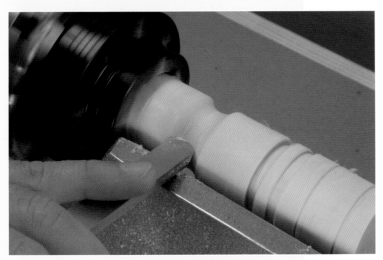

Sanding a cove

If all went well cutting or scraping your cove, little or even no sanding will be required. If you did experience some tear-out, you can sand a smooth profile by wrapping a piece of sandpaper around a dowel that's slightly narrower than the diameter of the cove, as shown in the bottom photo. Sand from below so that you can watch the profile on the top edge of the cove as shown.

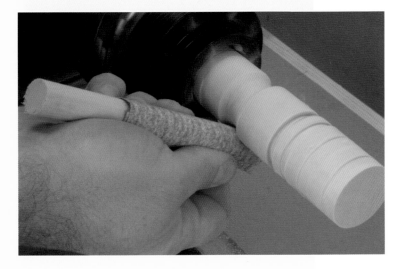

Turning a Bead

Beads are another type of decorative accent common on many turnings. Although not quite as simple as coves, they're fun to make.

Lay out the bead
To turn a bead, start by laying out its width and position. Use the same techniques that you used for coves and press a pencil into the blank to define the shoulders of the bead as shown in the top photo.

Rough out the bead
Next, because a bead sits proud of the surface of the blank, you'll need to remove stock on both sides of the bead to provide clearance for your turning tools, as shown in the middle photo. You can do this with a gouge, skew chisel, or flat-nose scraper as shown here. Check the diameter on both sides of the bead with a caliper to make sure they're uniform.

Define one side
A bead is turned with a skew chisel, using virtually the opposite technique that you'd use to cut a cove. Start with the chisel held vertically at the center of the bead. Then press in and twist your wrist to peel off shavings as shown in the bottom photo. Slow down as you approach the spindle surface. Here again, with practice, you can usually turn one-half of a small bead in a single pass (depending on its radius). Large coves will require several passes to remove the larger amount of stock, but the technique is the same. You can use a gouge instead, but you'll have to rotate the tool as you near the surface to keep the corners from digging into the spindle.

Define the other side

Just as with a cove, it's best to turn a bead as two halves. Reposition the skew chisel so that the cut will once again start at the center of the bead, and this time rotate the chisel in the opposite direction to define the other half of the bead, as shown in the top photo. If the two halves don't match, trim the offending side with light paring cuts, using the same technique as you did to make the bead.

Undercut to create more detail

A classic way to make a bead "pop" or stand out more is to slightly undercut each side of the bead. The tip of a skew chisel held flat against the tool rest as shown in the middle photo is an easy way to do this. Alternatively, for more of a cutting action, hold the skew point down vertically on the tool rest and make a slicing cut into the side of the bead, starting about one-third up from the bottom and stopping at the surface of the blank.

BEADING TOOLS

Have to cut a lot of beads? Consider purchasing a special type of scraper called a beading tool, or beader. A beading tool has a pointed tip that defines the limit of the bead. To each side of the point, the tip is shaped in a quarter-round to define one side of the bead. To use a beader, simply push it into the rotating stock and it'll quickly define the bead as shown in the photo at right. With a little practice, you can shape various-sized beads.

Turning a Tenon

One or both ends of many spindle-turned parts will terminate with a tenon to fit in a mortise drilled into other parts of the project, such as the cross spindles of a chair. The only tricky part to turning a tenon is sizing it correctly to fit the intended mortise.

Define the shoulder

The first step in turning a tenon is to lay out the length of the tenon and then define the shoulder of the tenon with a parting tool and calipers set to the rough diameter, as shown in the top photo. It's best to set the calipers slightly wider than the desired tenon diameter to leave sufficient stock for final shaping and cleanup.

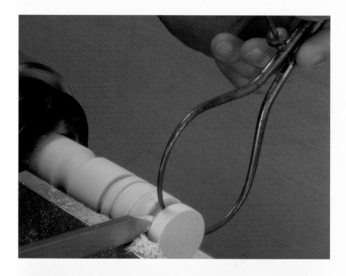

Remove tenon waste

Once you've defined the shoulder, go ahead and remove the bulk of the waste with a gouge as shown in the middle photo. Take care to cut only as deep as the parting tool has cut, or you'll end up with a too-small tenon. It's best to start at the parting tool kerf and work toward the end of the tenon as shown to keep from accidentally damaging or nicking the shoulder, which generally needs to remain square.

Wrench tip

Although calipers work well for defining the desired tenon diameter, you may have a tool in your toolbox that will do a better job—an open-ended wrench like the one shown in the bottom photo. Open-ended wrenches have two advantages over calipers. First, if you want a $9/16"$ tenon, grab a $9/16"$ wrench—it'll be dead-on accurate. Second, the wider inside surfaces of the wrench jaws allow you to check a longer portion of the tenon at the same time. The easiest way to do this is to position the wrench as if it were a set of calipers and then make light cuts on the tenon with a parting tool or square-nose scraper. As soon as the wrench slips over the tenon, it's sized perfectly.

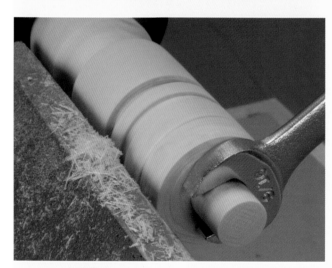

Parting Off

A parting tool is actually a special scraper that's designed to prepare a spindle for removal from the lathe, or to actually remove a part or "part off" a portion of a workpiece held in a chuck (such as removing the top of a turned box held in a scroll or screw chuck). Safety Note: If you're preparing a spindle for removal, take care to leave sufficient stock so that the workpiece is still rigid. We've seen novice turners reduce the spindle diameter so far that the workpiece started to flex, then chatter, then fly off the lathe. This just isn't necessary, as you'll most likely cut the waste off with a saw anyway. What's one or two more saw strokes compared to possibility of a flying spindle?

With parting tool and supporting hand

The same tool rest position and technique you used for scrapers is similar to that used with a parting tool. The only thing that's different is that you can present the tool to the workpiece so it's centered on the workpiece and then begin the cut. Then press down as you tilt the handle up to begin scraping. This will cut a kerf the same width as the parting tool in the workpiece. If you're parting off an unsupported piece like that shown in the left photo, use one hand to "catch" the workpiece as it separates—just take care to keep your fingers away from the tool rest to prevent a nasty pinch.

Parting off a lid

If you're turning a lidded box (see pages 176–180), you'll find it necessary to part the lid off the blank as shown here in the top right photo. Use the same technique for parting off parts described above,

except that if you have sufficient stock, consider widening the kerf that the parting tool makes by taking a series of light cuts (about $1/4$" to $1/2$" deep), alternating back and forth to create a double-wide kerf. This extra clearance prevents the tip of the parting tool from heating up because of the friction, which it is particularly wont to do on a deep cut, such as parting off a lid. With a single kerf, the sides of the tool tip are constantly rubbing against the workpiece. If you take a single, deep cut, it's quite possible to heat the tip to the point that you'll remove the temper from the steel.

Parting with a skew chisel

Parting off can also be done with a skew chisel by inverting it so the point is down, as shown in the bottom right photo. This is particularly useful when the remaining shoulder or face needs to be clean and smooth. Parting tools, even when sharp, tend

to tear the wood and leave a rough surface. A properly sharpened skew chisel will leave a smooth surface that needs little or no sanding.

Preparing for Faceplate Work

Faceplates are a type of chuck that allow you to turn plates, platters, bowls, and trays. Instead of gripping the wood like a 4-jaw or scroll chuck, the workpiece is screwed to the face of the plate via holes in the plate.

Preparing a blank

To make a round blank, first find the center and then use a compass to draw the circle size you want. It's easy to set a compass with a steel rule. Just set the steel point into the etched graduation at the 1" mark and then adjust the drawing point to the desired radius (plus 1"). Although the steel point of a compass generally does an adequate job of holding its place, we've found that making a slight starter hole with an awl helps keep the point from wandering as the compass is rotated to mark the circle, as shown in the top photo.

Rough cut on band saw

Once you've drawn the shape, cut it out with a band saw (as shown in the middle photo), saber saw, or scroll saw. As a general rule, it's best to stay on the waste side of your marked line to make sure you don't end up with a blank that's too small.

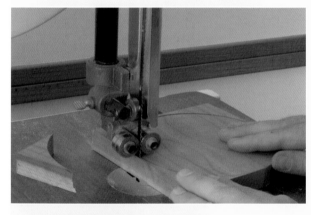

Attach the faceplate

Before attaching the faceplate to the blank, it's best to drill shank holes in the blank for the screws. Here again, dense woods will benefit the most from this, as screws driven in without shank holes tend to snap off. Make sure to use the largest-diameter screws that can fit through the holes in the faceplate, and drive them flush with the back of the faceplate. If the blank is large, heavy, or of green wood, use as many as screws as there are holes—the last thing you want is a blank flying off the lathe.

Mount onto lathe

All that's left is to mount the face-plate with blank onto the lathe. To do this, first lock the spindle in place, if there's a spindle lock; if there isn't, have the spindle wrench on hand to keep it from rotating, as shown in the top photo. Then just thread the faceplate onto the head-stock spindle so it bottoms out and is firmly in place. Depending on your faceplate, it

may or may not have flats on the hub that you can use to tighten it onto the headstock spindle. This is rarely necessary, as the rotation of the blank will be opposite the thread rotation, and as soon as you start turning, the impact of the tool on the blank will tighten it onto the headstock spindle sufficiently. Make sure to release the spindle lock before turning on the lathe.

FACEPLATE RINGS

Faceplate rings are a lathe accessory that can save you a lot of time and headache if you turn a lot—particularly if you work with green wood. A faceplate ring is a steel collar with holes in it for mounting to a blank. What makes these special is that the inside edge of the ring is beveled to match the bevel on the jaws of a scroll chuck as shown in the drawing at right. In use, a ring is attached to a blank and then mounted onto a scroll chuck for turning (see page 83 for more on using a scroll chuck).

This may not seem like a big deal—why not just use a faceplate? The thing is, production turners who turn green wood typically turn a piece to a rough shape and then let it dry before finish-turning. This means mounting and remounting the workpiece, and it's difficult to re-center a piece on the lathe in the same position as it was first turned. Not a problem if you use a faceplate ring. Just attach the ring and leave it be. When the blank is dry, it can be quickly and accurately remounted on the lathe. Production turners have stacks of faceplate rings, as this is much less expensive than leaving multiple scroll chucks attached to a workpiece.

CROSS SECTION

Scroll Chuck

Faceplate Ring Attached to Scroll Chuck

Blank

Screws Attach Ring to Blank

Attach ring to blank. Attach a faceplate ring to a blank just as you would a faceplate; make sure to use all the holes in the ring.

Mount on lathe. Contract the jaws of the scroll chuck until the ring fits over the jaws, then expand them to tighten; you can remove and replace the workpiece as often as you'd like and it'll always be perfectly centered.

Once you've mounted your faceplate/blank onto the lathe, the next step is to position the tool rest. How you do this will depend on if you're working on the rim or the face of the blank.

Tool rest position for rim work

To position a tool rest for working on the rim, first loosen the tool rest base clamp and slide the tool rest over so its base is as close to the blank as possible without interfering with it. Before you lock down the base clamp, rotate the blank to make sure it clears the tool rest. Reposition as necessary and lock down the base clamp.

All that's left is to adjust the height and angle of the tool rest. In most cases, you'll want the edge of the tool rest parallel with the blank; the only time you'll angle the tool rest is if you've already trued up the rim and have started shaping the edge. Here's where you'd angle the tool rest to match the angle of the rim so that the rest could be as close as possible to the blank in order to provide optimum support.

As to the height, there's as much debate on this as there is with spindle turning. For gouge work you'll generally want the tool rest somewhere near the center of the blank as shown in the top left photo. This will depend on the tool you're using, your stance, and the diameter of the blank. Tool rest position can vary by 1/8" or so either way, as shown in the top right drawing.

Tool rest position for face work

Use the same procedure described above to position the tool rest for working on the face of the blank. Here again, keep the tool rest as close as possible to the blank and adjust the height so the tool rest is roughly centered on the blank, as shown in the bottom photo. The idea here is to keep the cutting edge of the tool near the centerline of the blank. Since tools vary substantially in height, the tool rest will have to be adjusted accordingly.

RIM WORK TOOL REST POSITION

Position Tool Rest 1/8" below Center of Blank

Faceplate-Mounted Blank

1/8" Gap between Tool Rest and Blank

Tool Rest

SIDE VIEW

Truing the Rim

After you've adjusted the tool rest position, height, and angle, you're ready to true up the rim. We generally do this before proceeding to the face, as variations in the rim caused by cutting the blank to rough shape (or if the blank was mounted off-center) will cause the workpiece to wobble. Wobble can lead to vibration, which causes poor turning conditions. Once the rim is true, it can be shaped (page 68) and then the face can be trued and shaped (pages 70–71). Note: If the blank you're working on is large, consider bringing over the tailstock for added support until you've trued the rim.

Tool position
As with any turning operation, proper tool position is with the bevel rubbing against the workpiece while resting on the tool rest, as shown in the upper left

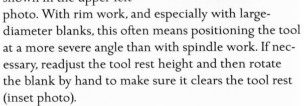

photo. With rim work, and especially with large-diameter blanks, this often means positioning the tool at a more severe angle than with spindle work. If necessary, readjust the tool rest height and then rotate the blank by hand to make sure it clears the tool rest (inset photo).

With a gouge
Now you can turn on the lathe and start truing the edge. If the blank is out of round or slightly off-center, start by taking very light cuts, as shown in the top right photo. The closer you get to round, the more aggressive you can cut. Just as with spindle work, you can check the blank for roundness with the chatter test. Simply rest your gouge lightly on top of the blank as shown in the inset photo. Any up-and-down motion or clicking means it's not round yet.

With a scraper
You can also true the rim of a blank up quickly with a scraper—just realize that the surface will likely be rougher than that of a gouge. To do this, adjust the tool rest as needed to position the scraper slightly below the centerline of the blank. Then with the scraper blade tilted down, take a series of light cuts as shown in the bottom right photo. If you want a smooth surface, burnish a fresh burr on the scraper (see page 154) and take very light cuts.

Shaping the Rim

Once the rim is true on your faceplate blank, the next step is typically to shape the rim. Whether you do this next will depend on how true the face of your blank is. If it's a rough surface or warped, you'll most likely want to true up the face before shaping the rim. That's because any variation on the face can cause wobble, resulting in vibration.

With a gouge

Most turners tend to use a gouge for shaping a rim, as it cuts quickly and cleanly, leaving a smooth surface, as shown in the top photo. As you continue to shape the rim, stop frequently and readjust the position of the tool rest to keep it as close as possible to the workpiece. Angle the tool rest as needed also to keep it close to the profile. When you stop and do this, it's also a good time to check the profile against a pattern or template; see below.

With a scraper

You can also use a scraper to shape a rim as shown in the middle photo. Here again, the tool rest will need to be repositioned so it's slightly below the centerline. Hold the scraper with the blade tilted down and take light cuts. Notice that with a fine burr on the end of the scraper, you can get whisper-thin shavings like those shown in the middle photo.

Check the profile

One challenge to shaping the rim or edge of a blank is that it's not easy to match it to a given profile or pattern. That's because you can't use a parting tool and caliper to define transition points as you would when spindle-turning (it'd take a heck of a big caliper to fit around most faceplate work). An alternative that we've found works well is to make a "negative" template from a piece of cardboard. To do this, trace the desired edge profile on the cardboard and cut out the profile. This way you can place the template on the rim periodically to see how the shaping is coming along, as shown in the bottom photo.

Scraping the Face

When you're happy with the shape of the rim on your faceplate-mounted workpiece, you can turn your attention to the face. The face can be shaped either by scraping, as shown here, or with cutting tools as described on page 70–71. To get a good surface when scraping, make sure to sharpen and burnish the scraper as described on pages 144 and 154, respectively.

Start at the rim

In most cases you'll want to start shaping a face with a scraper by quickly truing up the face (if you haven't done this previously). A couple of light passes with a round- or square-nose scraper will usually do the job. Then you can start shaping the face. As a general rule, you'll want to start near the rim and work your way toward the center, as shown in the top photo. Most turners find that this provides better control, as it's quite easy to plow right through the rim if you turn in the reverse direction.

Work toward the center

You'll notice that the sound of the cutting action will change dramatically as you near the center of the blank. There are two reasons for this. One has to do with the relationship of the tool to the diameter of the blank. The farther out toward the rim, the faster the wood is moving, because of the greater circumference; closer in means slower-moving wood (middle photo). Second, the wood near the center is supported fully by the faceplate versus the unsupported wood near the rim. Because of this, you'll generally want to push the scraper slower along the tool rest as you near the center to keep the cutting action uniform.

Flats

A flat-nose scraper is one of the easiest ways to create a flat uniform surface on a faceplate-mounted blank. Just make sure to keep the edge of the scraper parallel to the face of the blank as you slide it along the tool rest, as shown in the bottom photo. To prevent catches, it's also a good idea to file or grind off the very corners of the scraper as described on page 146.

Shaping the Face

Shaping the face of a faceplate-mounted workpiece with a gouge is very similar to the method described for a scraper (page 69). There are, however, a couple of important differences. One is that a gouge is much more apt to catch near the edge. That's why it's important for beginning woodturners to establish a starting point for the gouge as described below. Second, unlike a scraper, which lies flat on the tool rest at all times, a gouge is rotated through the cut to present the best cutting edge to the work to get the cleanest cut.

tip into the wood and how fast or slow you slide it along the tool rest. Additionally, if you're using a fingernail gouge, you can take a very aggressive cut by angling the gouge to present one of the wing edges ground on the side of the gouge to the workpiece.

Use a parting tool or skew to create a lip
Because the speed at the rim is so fast, it's very easy for a gouge to catch the grain as it comes in contact with the work-piece and literally go in the wrong direction. That is, it can cut away from the center instead of toward it—and this can be disastrous to an edge that you carefully sculpted earlier. To prevent this from happening, give the gouge a starting point by cutting a lip near the rim where you want to start cutting. You can do this with a skew chisel on its side (as shown in the upper left photo) or with a parting tool. In most cases, a 1/8"-deep lip or recess will do just fine.

Working from the rim in
Start your cut by placing the gouge near the rim (or in the lip as described above if you've cut one). Roll the tool slightly as shown in the top right photo to produce more of a shearing cut, and gently press forward. As soon as it begins cutting, slide the gouge slowly along the tool rest. How aggressive a cut you make will depend on how hard you press the gouge

Leave a center cone
As you cut toward the center of the blank, it's best to leave a center portion unturned in the form of a cone as shown in the middle right photo. This cone will help keep the blank balanced because of its centered mass. And a better balanced blank means less vibration, which leads to better cutting action and smoother surfaces.

CUTTING DIRECTION AND SEQUENCE

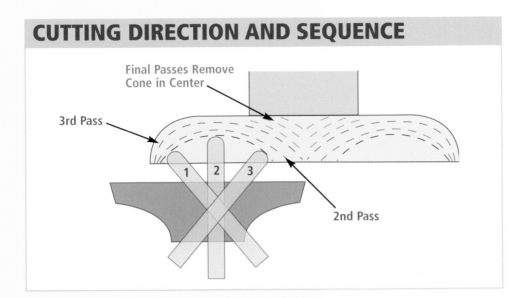

Final Passes Remove
Cone in Center

3rd Pass

1 2 3

2nd Pass

Direction and sequence
After you've made a first pass with your gouge and have left a cone-shaped center section, continue taking additional passes as illustrated in the top drawing. When you've turned the recess to the desired depth, go back and remove the cone with a gouge or flat-nose scraper.

VARIOUS TOOL POSITIONS

One of the things that takes some getting used to when turning the face of a blank is that your hand and tool positions will vary from tool to tool and from cut to cut, as shown in the photos below. This is one of the reasons why many beginning turners find the gouge more difficult to use than a scraper—a scraper basically only has one position on the tool rest—flat.

Long and strong gouge. Although the profile on this long and strong gouge is similar to that of a standard gouge, it can't be held at as acute an angle as the standard gouge because your body ends up in the way of the tool handle.

Roughing gouge. Because the corners on the square end of a roughing gouge are prone to catches, the tool is held nearly perpendicular to the face of the blank.

Standard gouge. A standard gouge has an oval profile on the end and so can be angled much further away from perpendicular.

Sanding

Although every woodturner (and every woodworker, for that matter) would like to say they never need to sand a part, it's a fact of life. Even with the sharpest tools and best techniques, you'll find it necessary to sand surfaces to remove imperfections—particularly when working with high-figured or squirrelly grain.

Remove the tool rest

The most important thing to remember when you need to sand a part is to get the tool rest out of the way. If possible, remove it from the lathe; otherwise position it as far from the workpiece as possible, as shown in the top left photo. A serious pinch point exists between a tool rest and a workpiece, and because sanding generally requires holding the sandpaper with your hand against the revolving wood, you don't want the tool rest anywhere near your fingers. Get into this habit now and your fingers will always be grateful.

Proper hand position

Now although you can technically sand from above or below a workpiece, there are a couple of good reasons why you may prefer sanding from below, as shown in the bottom photo. The biggest reason you may like this is that you can see what you're sanding. Sanding on top of the workpiece often obscures the workpiece and it's real easy to

sand away a fine detail. Second, since the workpiece is rotating toward you at the bottom, it's easier to keep the sandpaper pressed against the spinning workpiece. For most turning we'll start with 120- or 150-grit and work our way up to 220- or 280-grit, depending on the finish desired.

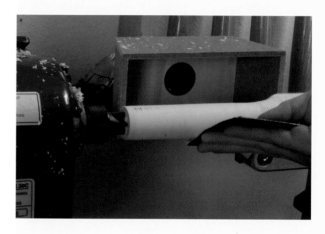

Dust collection

Turning creates quite a mess with shavings, but there's nothing like a little sanding to quickly generate a cloud of messy and harmful dust. Protect your lungs and keep your shop clean by using some form of dust collection—even if it's a fan covered with a filter to suck dust away from the lathe and trap it in the filter. Better yet, use a dust hood hooked up to a dust-collection system or shop vacuum. Plans for the shop-built hood shown in the upper right photo can be found on pages 110–115.

Sanding block for flats

If you find that you need to sand a flat area, consider using a small scrap of wood as a sanding block, as shown in the top left photo. Not only will this keep your fingers from overheating from the friction generated from sanding, but it'll also help create a uniformly flat surface that's hard to get with just your fingers serving as backing for the sandpaper.

Turn off the lathe and sand

Because of the rotating nature of the workpiece, odds are that even with careful sanding, you'll still end up with some circular scratches on the surface of your workpiece. A simple and effective way to remove these scratches is to turn off the lathe and sand by hand, following the grain, as shown in the top right photo. You may find it useful to engage the spindle lock to keep the workpiece from rotating as you sand.

PNEUMATIC SANDING DRUMS

A sanding accessory that many lathe owners find useful is a pneumatic sanding drum like the one shown in the bottom photo. These drums are designed to mount between centers on the lathe to handle a variety of sanding tasks. What's really nice about these is that you can control the "give" of the drum by inflating or deflating the bladder in between the ends of the drum. A standard air fitting like you'd find on a bicycle tire allows anyone with a hand pump to vary the amount of cushion on the surface of the drum.

Finishing

One of our favorite things about working on the lathe is that you can often go from rough blank to finished project without removing the workpiece from the lathe. This means the lathe is the only stationary power tool out there that allows you to apply a finish to the workpiece as you near completion.

Burnishing tip

Once you're done sanding (if necessary), consider using an old turner's trick before you apply a finish—burnishing. This is nothing more than grabbing a handful of shavings and pressing them into the turning piece as shown in the upper left photo. This will produce a soft sheen on the surface and works particularly well with oily woods like teak. How much burnishing you get will depend on how hard you press the shavings into the spinning workpiece.

Apply paste wax

Paste wax is an excellent durable finish for many projects that is easy to maintain. One thing to keep in mind, however, is that paste wax generally doesn't create the high gloss that some other finishes do. But if you're after a nice mellow glow, paste wax is the answer. What's really nice about a paste wax finish is how easy it is to apply. With the lathe off, simply dip the tip of a rag in the wax and apply it to the workpiece as shown in the middle photo. Take care to keep the wax away from any parts (like tenons) that will need to be glued up later, as it will interfere with the bond. ShopTip: Consider protecting parts to be glued up by wrapping masking tape around them to keep them finish-free.

Buff and repeat as needed

After you've applied the paste wax to the desired areas, wipe off any extra wax and then turn on the lathe. Then just press a clean, soft cloth up against the spinning workpiece to buff it to a soft sheen as shown in the bottom photo. Make sure to keep the rag away from drive centers and chucks, which have a wicked tendency to grab the rag and pull it (and possibly your fingers) into the center or chuck. If you're looking for more of a sheen, stop the lathe, apply another coat of wax, and buff again. Repeat as needed until the desired sheen is achieved.

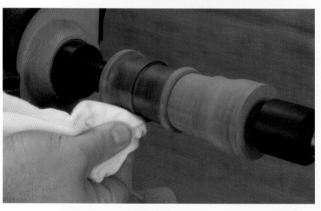

LIQUID FRICTION FINISHES

There's a new breed of lathe-applied finishes out there that we really like. Liquid friction finishes, like the HUT Crystal Coat finish shown here, are a snap to apply. They are formulated to be the final and only finish you need to apply to a project. (For more on Crystal Coat, visit HUT's website at www.hutproducts.com.) You can apply the finish with a brush or a cloth.

Apply with a brush. To apply a liquid finish with a brush, you can either squirt some finish on the workpiece, as shown in the top photo, or dispense some into a disposable cup and dip the brush into the cup. We've found that it's easiest to simply squirt and brush. This technique is especially useful when finishing larger projects.

Apply with a cloth. Smaller projects and parts lend themselves to cloth application. Just squeeze a couple drops of finish on a clean, soft cloth and apply this to the workpiece with the lathe off to get an even distribution, as shown in the middle photo. Rotate the workpiece as needed to coat the entire surface.

Power-buff. Now you can turn the lathe on and apply a dry, clean, soft cloth to the spinning workpiece with moderate pressure, moving steadily back and forth over its surface, as shown in the bottom photo. Heat from the resulting friction will create a gloss finish in seconds.

4 Advanced Lathe Techniques

There are a couple of things that separate advanced from beginning techniques in woodturning. The first is the tools involved. Most beginning woodturning can be accomplished with the tools and accessories that come standard with most every lathe. As your skill level progresses and you start to push the boundaries of these tools and accessories, you'll come to realize that you need additional equipment. This new equipment can be anything from long and strong tools to advanced chucks like a scroll or 4-jaw chuck with various jaws.

Second, a higher level of confidence is required to take on a project that requires turning a big, heavy blank with the tool extended past the tool rest, as when turning a bowl. A bowl is something a turner should tackle only after feeling comfortable with the lathe, the tools, and basic techniques such as spindle turning and simple faceplate turning. In this chapter, we'll show you how to turn a bowl, save wood with a coring system, tackle segmented turning, and more.

Ah, the joy of turning a bowl. One of woodturning's greatest pleasures. There's nothing quite like long, thin shavings curling off a blank as you anxiously watch the bowl take shape under the gouge.

Turning a Bowl: The Exterior

There are a couple of reasons why bowl turning is generally classified as an advanced technique. First, turning a bowl usually means working with larger and heavier blanks. This in itself can be a challenge, especially on a smaller lathe. (Note: Because bowl blanks are typically large, it's always best to get them as round as possible before mounting them on the lathe to help reduce vibration.) Second, turning a bowl means working with a couple different kinds of chucks that most beginning turners don't own. And finally, turning the interior of a bowl often means extending the turning tool—whether it's a gouge or a scraper—well past the tool rest, and this requires additional skills not needed for the bulk of spindle and simple faceplate turning.

Attaching a blank with a scrap block

If the screw holes will be an issue, an alternate way to mount a blank to a faceplate is to first attach a disposable scrap block to the face of the blank, as shown in the top photo. As a general rule, we'll sandwich a sheet of kraft paper between the two to make separating the blank from the scrap easier. Once the glue has dried—preferably overnight—attach the faceplate to the scrap as you'd attach it to a blank.

Attach the blank to a faceplate

There are a number of ways to prepare a blank for turning a bowl, but we tend to start by attaching a blank to a faceplate, as shown in the bottom left photo. The idea here is to turn the exterior and bottom of the bowl first, then transfer this to a scroll chuck for turning the interior of the bowl. The advantage of this method is that since you'll be removing the bulk of the wood in the interior, you can drive deep screws into it to attach the faceplate. In our opinion, this is the strongest way to mount a blank for turning. Remember to use as many holes as there are in the faceplate to secure the blank.

Mount the blank on the lathe

With the faceplate secured, you can mount the blank on the lathe. Simply screw the faceplate onto the headstock spindle as shown in the bottom right photo. Lock or hold the spindle in place to make sure the hub on the faceplate butts firmly up against the headstock spindle. No need to over-tighten here, as your beginning cuts on the exterior will tighten the faceplate onto the spindle.

USING A SCREW CHUCK

For smaller bowl blanks and turned boxes, a screw chuck can be used in lieu of a faceplate. A screw chuck is basically a sleeve that threads onto the headstock spindle with a screw protruding from its business end. Most screw chucks will grip a workpiece surprisingly well, plus their small size makes it easy to shape the full length of the blank—something that's hard to do with larger-diameter faceplates.

Drill a pilot hole. To use a screw chuck, start by preparing the blank. Make sure the end that the chuck will screw onto is square so the blank won't end up angled on the chuck. Then mark the center of the blank and drill a pilot hole for the screw chuck—consult the owner's manual for your screw chuck for the recommended drill bit size. Also, it's best to drill this hole on a drill press (as shown in the top photo) instead of with a portable drill, to ensure that the hole is perpendicular to the end of the blank.

Screw the chuck to the blank. Now you can screw the chuck to the blank as shown in the middle photo. If you are screwing into end grain, which tends to be weak, consider drilling a hole near the end of the blank for a dowel. Drill about two-thirds of the way through the thickness of the blank and then cut a dowel to fit (we use ½" or larger dowels). Tap the dowel into the hole that you drilled in the side so its grain is perpendicular to the end grain. This way when you screw the chuck to the blank, the screw will bite into the long grain of the dowel to hold the blank firmly in place.

Mount the chuck on the lathe. With the blank attached to the screw chuck, you can mount it on the lathe as shown in the bottom photo. Thread the screw chuck onto the spindle so it butts up against the headstock. Here again, there's no need to overtighten, as your first cuts will lock the screw chuck onto the spindle.

True the blank

Once the bowl blank is mounted onto the lathe, it's a good idea to true up the blank to minimize vibration, as shown in the top photo. A roughing or spindle gouge works best for this. Note that many pro turners don't bother with this stage and simply start by shaping the exterior of the bowl. This works fine if you feel confident in doing this and can shape the exterior without the need for layout and at least a partial definition of the shape, as described below.

Lay out the desired shape

After truing up the bowl blank, the next step is to lay out the shape on the blank, using a pattern or rule and a pencil as shown in the middle photo. At a minimum you'll want to mark the lip or edge of the bowl and the base or foot. If there are transition areas that can be defined where a curve or detail starts and stops, mark these as well.

Define the shape

With the pattern laid out, go ahead and define the diameters at each point with a parting tool as shown in the bottom photo. The diameters of smaller bowls can be checked with a large caliper. Larger diameters can be check by measuring the depth of the kerf or groove with a metal rule and subtracting double this from the overall diameter of the blank to find the diameter of the blank where the kerf has been cut.

Rough out the shape

As soon as you're done defining any critical diameters of the bowl's exterior with a parting tool, you can switch to a spindle or fingernail gouge and begin roughing out the shape, as shown in the top photo. The object here is to remove waste on each side of the kerfs to match the specified diameters while following the basic pattern for the bowl. Take care here to check your pattern frequently to make sure you don't remove too much stock.

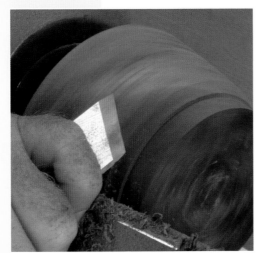

Finish the shape

With the exterior shaped to the rough pattern, go ahead and turn the exterior smooth. For slow, gradual curves like those on the bowl shown here, we'll switch to a wide skew chisel to get a very smooth surface, as shown in the middle photo. For less gradual curves, use a sharp spindle or fingernail gouge or a freshly burnished round-nose scraper.

Turn the bottom

After the exterior of the bowl has been smoothed, switch the tool rest to the face of the blank and turn the bottom smooth, as shown in the bottom photo. Just about any gouge can be used for this, as no curves are involved. We used a roughing gouge, but you could use a spindle gouge, fingernail gouge, or bowl gouge. Alternatively, a flat-nose scraper does a good job of creating a flat bottom.

Lay out a recess for a scroll chuck

The last thing to do to complete the exterior of the bowl is to lay out and cut a recess in the bottom for a scroll chuck. This will allow you to transfer the blank to the scroll chuck so you can turn the interior. To do this, you'll first need to know the gripping range of your scroll chuck. This will vary by the brand and by which jaws you are using. The more sets of accessory jaws you have, the greater the size range of the recess. We generally lay out the recess so there's at least 1/2" or more material left at the perimeter of the base, as shown in the top photo. This will leave sufficient material to hold up against the powerful jaws of the chuck. As a general rule, the larger the blank, the deeper the recess and the more material you should leave at the perimeter.

Rough out the recess

After you've laid out the recess, go ahead and remove the waste inside the marked perimeter. We like to first define the perimeter with a parting tool, as shown in the middle photo. Then go back with a spindle gouge or flat-nose scraper to remove the bulk of the waste and create a flat bottom in the recessed area. For smaller bowls, a recess depth of between 1/4" and 3/8" is usually sufficient. Larger and heavier bowls will benefit from deeper recesses—how deep will depend on how much stock you want to leave at the base or foot of the bowl and on the length of the chuck jaws. Jaws designed specifically for gripping bowls are both stouter and longer than conventional jaws (see page 28 for more on bowl jaws).

Define the dovetail lip

Since the jaws of a scroll chuck are angled, you need to create a recess with an inside edge that matches the angle of the chuck jaws. The most reliable way to do this is to use a dovetail scraper specifically designed for this (see page 35). Most turners can't justify this special tool and simply use a skew chisel on edge to cut the angled lip as shown in the bottom photo. With a little practice, you'll be able to cut a matching angle with ease.

USING A SCROLL CHUCK

A scroll chuck is the perfect way to safely grip a bowl blank for turning the interior. Not only does this let you grip the blank, but it also leaves a nicely finished bottom. To use one, you'll have to first turn a recess in the bottom of the blank, as illustrated in the drawing at right.

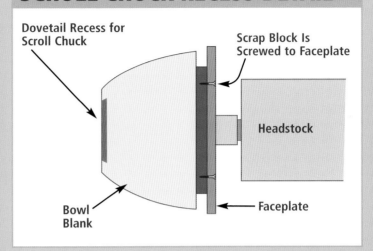

Dovetail Recess for Scroll Chuck

Scrap Block Is Screwed to Faceplate

Headstock

Bowl Blank

Faceplate

Adding the jaws. Because a scroll chuck can only open and close over a small range, multiple sets of jaws are required to handle a variety of recess sizes. This means that you'll often be faced with changing jaws. This is simple to do, but must be done correctly for the jaws to grip the blank securely. The jaws on scroll chucks will have stepped locater rings on the back of the jaws that fit into grooved sections on the jaw slides. It's important that these two mesh together perfectly. To help with this, both the jaws and the slides are numbered as shown in the top photo. This is to ensure that you get the jaws on the chuck the way they are intended.

Friction-tight screws. Once you've matched up a jaw to a jaw slide and positioned it on the slide so the mounting holes align, you can add the screws as shown in the middle photo. (Note that some chuck manufacturers suggest adding a drop of light machine oil to the threads of each screw before screwing them into the slides, to prevent the screws from locking onto the jaw.) The heads of the screws generally accept an Allen wrench. What's really important here is that you need to thread the screws in so they're just barely friction-tight—DO NOT tighten them fully. Once all the jaws and screws are in place, proceed to the next step.

Close the jaws and then tighten. To make sure the jaws grip a recess uniformly around its perimeter, first wind the jaws closed with a wrench or scroll bars until the jaws butt firmly against each other. Then tighten the screws fully as shown in the bottom photo. Now the chuck is ready for use.

Turning a Bowl: The Interior

Much of turning involves hollowing or removing waste with a gouge. Entire books have been written on bowl turning to cover this challenging but rewarding pastime. Some of the best advice we can give about turning the interior of a bowl is to give it a shot and keep at it. The more you practice, the better you'll get, the higher your confidence level, and the better your bowls will become. Plan on wasting some scrap wood to achieve this. And know that odds are, you'll end up with a few catches and some scarred wood. But don't give up—creating a bowl out of a block of wood from start to finish on a lathe is one of woodworking's joyful and intensely creative pleasures.

right photo. Now go back and make a slightly deeper cut. The idea here is to make a series of hollowing or scooping cuts that will leave a cone in the center of the bowl, as illustrated in the drawing below. This cone will help stabilize the hole and hold down vibration as you continue hollowing.

Start at the rim

We do most of our hollowing work with a $1/2$" or $3/8$" fingernail gouge. Although you might think to just jab the gouge into the workpiece straight on, you'll find that you'll get a cleaner cut by presenting the tool to the workpiece at a slight angle, as shown in the middle left photo. This is known as a shear cut and it creates a much cleaner cut—just as if you skewed a hand plane while planing. Since the cutting action takes place more on the side of the cutting tip instead of the end, this technique does require some practice. But keep at it—you'll be rewarded with flowing shavings and glass-smooth surfaces. We also suggest beginning bowl turners create a starting point for their gouge as described on page 70. Start your cut at the rim and work toward the center.

Work toward the center

As you work toward the center with your gouge, stop before you reach the center, as shown in the top

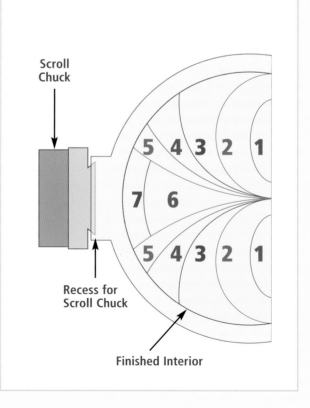

BOWL INTERIOR CUTTING SEQUENCE

Scroll Chuck

5 4 3 2 1

7 6

5 4 3 2 1

Recess for Scroll Chuck

Finished Interior

Continue removing stock

Continue shaping the interior of the bowl by making successively deeper cuts, as shown in the top photo. With time you'll develop a rhythmic swaying, pivoting movement that will become natural the more you do it. A good way to gain confidence while turning deeper into the bowl is to turn the lathe off and have a helper rotate the headstock handwheel as you make a cut. This will allow you to watch how the gouge tip contacts the wood and will provide feedback on the best way to position it. If you're using a fingernail gouge with wide wings sharpened on the sides, you'll find that you'll be rotating or rolling the tool as you make your other movements.

Remove the center cone

Once you've completed the perimeter cuts, you can go back and remove the center cone. You can do this with a gouge or with a flat- or round-nose scraper as shown in the middle photo. Make a series of light cuts. Don't try and hog it all off in a couple of passes. Remember that this cone helps stabilize the bowl, and as it's removed, vibration can increase; so you don't want to be taking aggressive cuts here—unless you're amused with bowls flying off a chuck.

Finish-scrape if desired

With the cone removed, now is the time to finish-turn the interior of the bowl. This can be done with a gouge, but we prefer to finish-scrape the interior with a stout round-nose scraper as shown in the bottom photo. The advantage to using a heavy-duty scraper like this is that it's safer to extend a stout shank like these tools offer past the tool rest than it is with a narrower and more flexible gouge. Whichever tool you choose, make sure it's freshly honed or burnished and take very light cuts. If needed, sand the interior. For difficult-to-turn woods, consider power-sanding as described on page 97.

Using a Coring System

Anyone who's ever turned a bowl is well aware of how much of a blank ends up on the floor in the form of shavings. This is particularly hard to stomach when you've paid a lot for the blank. The folks at Oneway Manufacturing are well aware of this problem and have developed an amazing accessory for the lathe to literally "scoop" out the inside of a bowl in one piece so that you can turn another bowl (or bowls) from it. This patented system is called the Easy-Core system and it works extremely well—no more lost wood, dramatically less wood shavings and dust to clean up, plus much less wear and tear on your lathe and turning tools. For more on this system, see page 38 or visit Oneway's website at www.oneway.on.ca.

so that it fits under the gap in the bed, and with the base in rough position, thread the bolt into the clamp block. Oneway suggests making a template to insert between the base and the headstock to position the bed accurately before tightening it in place with the wrench provided, as shown in the top right photo. Alternatively, you leave the bolt friction-tight, and tighten it after adjusting the base to its final position once the cutter height has been established.

Mount the blank and turn the exterior

Before you can use the Easy-Core system, you'll need to mount an appropriate-sized bowl blank on the lathe and either turn the exterior of the bowl or simply true up the blank as we did here. (Consult the owner's manual or video that comes with the system on recommended blank sizes; the system accepts curved knives of varying diameters to create different-sized cores.) With large blanks like this, you'll want to use very slow speeds and a long and strong gouge, as shown in the middle left photo. This will reduce the weight of the blank and hold down vibration.

Mount the base to the lathe bed

Once you've got the exterior shaped or trued, the next step is to mount the base of the system onto your lathe. The base attaches to your bed via a bolt that threads into a clamp block. Oneway offers clamp blocks to fit most lathes. Slip the clamp block

CORING SEQUENCE

Scroll Chuck

1 2 3 4 5

Adjust the cutter height

With the base attached to the lathe bed, go ahead and adjust the height of the cutter. The cutting edge of the cutter should be centered on the center of your headstock spindle. The easiest way to do this is to first measure from the bed to the center of the spindle. Then insert the cutter in the appropriate column in the base (one is for the cutter, the other for the curved tool rest), and measure from the base to the cutter. If necessary, adjust the cutter up or down by loosening the lock nut on the bottom of the cutter and adjust the setscrew in or out as shown in the top photo. Snug the nut back up and insert the cutter in the holder and re-measure. Repeat as needed until the measurements match.

Adjust the cutter position

With the cutter height correct, you can loosen the nut that secures the base to the lathe bed so it's friction-tight. Then adjust the position of the base so the cutter hits the desired entry point on the bowl blank, as shown in the middle photo. Once in place, snug up the nut. (If you've cored before and have determined the exact position for the cutter and made a template, this step won't be necessary.)

Adjust the tool rest

The cutter is supported by a curved tool rest as it makes its cut. The tool rest fits into the tool rest column and needs to be adjusted to match the path of the cutter. The tool rest is held in place by a setscrew in tool rest holder column. Adjust the tool rest so it sits directly beneath the path of the cutter and so the cutter encounters just the slightest drag as it's pushed over the tool rest, as shown in the inset photo. Then lock the holder in place by tightening its nut on the base, and lock the tool rest in position in the tool rest holder by tightening the setscrew as shown in the bottom left photo.

Attach the handle

All that's left to do before you can begin coring is to attach the handle onto the rounded shank of the cutter as shown in the top photo. This is done by locking down a pair of setscrews in the handle with an Allen wrench as shown.

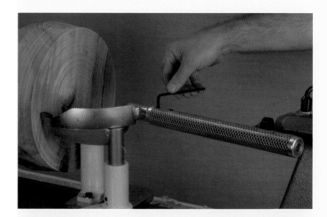

Begin coring

Now for the fun part. Turn on your lathe at a slow speed and pivot the cutter into the blank as shown in the middle photo. Take it easy here so the cutter can do its work. A firm grip and a steady feed rate are all it takes. If you feel you have to force the cutter into the blank, the removable tip on the end of the cutter should be removed and sharpened (see the owner's manual for sharpening details).

Clear out the chips frequently

As you core, stop frequently to back out the cutter and clear away chips. Although it's a relatively thin kerf you're cutting, you'll still generate a surprisingly large amount of shavings. The shavings shown in the bottom photo were creating by only cutting about an inch into the blank. Because the tip of the cutter is essentially captured between walls of spinning wood, heat can build up quickly. This is especially true when chips and shavings get lodged in the kerf. That's why it's so important to clear them frequently. With a little practice you'll be able both hear and feel when the chips start to build up and it's time to clear them. You can't over-clear the chips. The worst that'll happen is that it'll take you a little longer to cut the core—but the cutter tip will be happier.

Reposition the tool rest as needed

With continued cutting, the cutter will begin to extend too far past the tool rest and will begin to vibrate as it's unsupported. That's why you need to stop periodically and readjust the position of the tool rest so it supports the cutter. To do this, loosen the nut that secured the tool rest holder to the base and slide it forward so the tip of the tool rest extends into the curved kerf as shown in the inset photo. Take care that it's not contacting the wall of the blank, and then tighten the nut on the base as shown in the top left photo.

Bring the tailstock over and continue coring

If your tailstock is adjustable to the point where it can contact the blank, you're always better off adding this extra support. If your tailstock center can't extend far enough over the base of the coring system to contact the blank, consider purchasing one or more Morse taper extensions to allow it to reach (see page 15). Use the tailstock whenever possible, especially as you near the end of the cut when the cored section may break free (middle photo).

Remove the cored section

As you near the end of the cutter's path in the blank, you'll notice the sound of the cut changing dramatically. This is due to the fact that the diameter of the remaining wood that's holding the core in place is getting smaller and smaller. When it sounds like it's getting near the end, stop the lathe and insert a chisel in the kerf in the blank and gently pry out the core. Odds are that it will readily snap and pop out of the blank as shown in the bottom photo.

Split Turnings

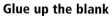

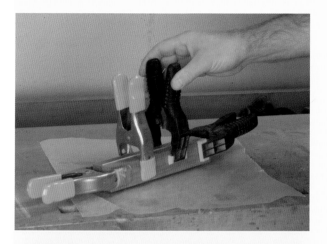

Split turning is a technique that lets you make identical appliqués for a project. The only thing that separates this from standard spindle turning is the preparation of the blank. Instead of using a single piece, two thinner sections are glued together. After the profile is turned, the pieces are split to produce identical half-sections, as shown in the top left photo.

Glue up the blank

To create a split turning, start by preparing two blanks of appropriate size. Then glue these together. To make it easier to separate the pieces once turning is complete, sandwich a piece of kraft paper between the two halves of the blank when you glue it up, as shown in the top right photo. Note that this technique can also be used to create four identical quarter profiles—just glue up four sections with kraft paper between each adjacent surface.

Turn the profile

Once the glue has dried—preferably overnight—prepare the blanks as you would any spindle blanks. Mark centers on the ends of the blank, drill clearance holes, and cut a pair of diagonal kerfs for the spurs of the drive center. Then mount the blank between centers and turn the profile as shown in the middle photo.

Split the blank in two

When the profile is complete, remove the blank and stand it on end. Place a chisel on the glue line between the halves and tap it with a hammer or mallet as shown in the bottom photo. If you used kraft paper, the blank should split easily in two. The kraft paper can then be easily removed with a hand scraper.

Using a Cole Jaw Chuck

If you don't like the idea of holding a bowl with a scroll chuck, you can still turn a bowl with a cleanly finished bottom. To do this, attach a blank to your faceplate and shape the exterior as much as possible. Then turn the inside of the bowl. So how do you finish the external profile and create a finished bottom? You use a set of accessory jaws for your scroll chuck, called cole jaws. These are basically a set of quarter sections of aluminum plate with a series of threaded holes that accept rubber bumpers. The bumpers are held in place with screws that fit into the threaded holes. As the chuck is opened and closed, the rubber bumpers grip the blank. (Alternatively, you can make a jam chuck for this; see pages 92–93.)

Mount the chuck on the lathe

To use a cole jaw chuck, start by mounting the cole jaws on the chuck. In most cases, the sections aren't numbered as standard jaws are, and you can attach them to any of the jaw slides. Then open the jaws fully and place your bowl blank on the chuck to locate the best position for the bumpers. Select a position that will allow them to grip the blank and thread all of the bumpers on the jaw sections at the appropriate circumference. Tighten the bumpers and then thread the chuck onto the headstock spindle, as shown in the bottom left photo.

Secure the bowl

Now you can place your bowl on the chuck and tighten it to grip the bowl, as shown in the top right photo. Take care to put only enough pressure on the bowl to firmly hold it in place. Too much pressure, and it's easy to crack the delicate sides of the bowl.

Turn the bottom

With the bowl secured to the chuck, you can shape the bottom and trim the exterior a bit if you want, as shown in the bottom right photo. Just keep in mind that you need to take very light cuts here with a sharp tool, as the only thing holding the bowl in place is the bumpers. Even a slight catch can cause the bowl to fly out of the chuck.

Using a Jam Chuck

A jam chuck is an alternative to the cole jaw chuck described on page 91. In our opinion a jam chuck will do a better job of holding a spinning bowl in place. The only disadvantage is that you typically have to make one for every individual bowl you turn. A jam chuck is just a scrap block attached to your faceplate. A kerf or groove is cut into the scrap to accept the lip or edge of your bowl. Then the bowl is literally jammed into the kerf and is held in place by the friction between the bowl and the scrap block, as illustrated in the top right drawing. Low-tech, yes, but inexpensive.

Attach a scrap to your faceplate

To make a jam chuck, start with a scrap of wood that's larger than the diameter of your bowl lip. In most cases, an inch or two larger is best, as this creates a strong edge after the recess is cut to hold the bowl without risk of the edge cracking. Cut the blank round and center it on your faceplate. Then secure it with as many screws as there are holes in the faceplate, as shown in the middle photo.

Cut a recess for the bowl's lip

Mount the faceplate-mounted scrap on the lathe by threading it onto the headstock spindle. Then position your tool rest to cut into the face of the scrap. If necessary, true up both the rim and the face to minimize vibration. Next measure the diameter of your bowl and the thickness of the sides. Transfer these to the face of the scrap block and then use a parting tool to cut a recess. If the sides of your bowl are angled or curved, angle the parting tool accordingly. Stop and check your progress often by checking to see whether the bowl will fit into the recess. In most cases a $1/2$"- to $5/8$"-deep recess will work fine.

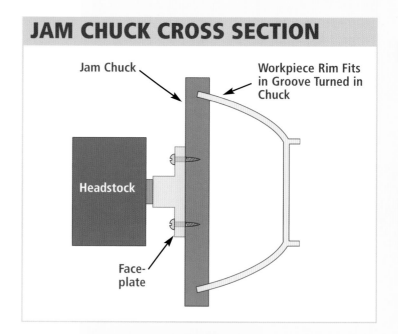

JAM CHUCK CROSS SECTION

Jam Chuck

Workpiece Rim Fits in Groove Turned in Chuck

Headstock

Face-plate

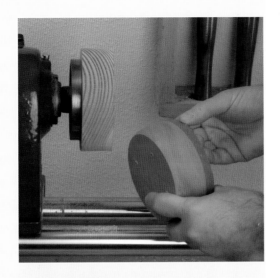

Shim with tape if necessary

If by chance you accidentally cut the recess too wide so the fit of the bowl is sloppy, often you can still use the jam chuck by wrapping a turn or two of masking tape around the edge of your bowl, as shown in the top photo. Masking tape works best here, as its surface is slightly dimpled, which provides a better grip. Shy away from duct tape, with its smooth shiny surface, which tends to slip in situations like this. After applying the tape, check the fit and apply more as needed.

Insert the bowl

With the recess cut and/or the bowl edge taped, you can jam the bowl into the recess in the chuck as shown in the middle photo. Take care to press the bowl in straight and not at an angle. Use slow, firm pressure to press it in place. Don't go overboard here or you'll have a tough time getting the bowl back out once you're done turning the bottom.

Turn the bottom

Once the bowl is jammed into the chuck, position your tool rest to turn the bottom. Before you turn on the lathe, give the headstock handwheel a full spin and watch the gap between the tool rest and the bowl bottom. It should be uniform in width as you rotate the bowl. If it isn't, the bowl is in at an angle and needs to be repositioned. When everything looks good, turn on the lathe and clean up the bottom as shown in the bottom photo. As with cole jaws, it's still best to take a series of light cuts to prevent an aggressive cut from pulling the bowl out of the chuck.

Segmented Turning

Segmented turning eliminates a few problems that every bowl turner faces. The first problem is the high cost of wood, particularly exotics. The second is the amount of wood that's typically wasted when turning. And the third has to do with grain. Unless you're turning an end-grain bowl, you'll encounter the end grain on the exterior in two places, which tends to be harder to cut cleanly. Segmented turning solves all of these by using small pieces of wood that are glued together to form a shell. Then another piece is recessed into the blank to form a bottom. Granted, this does limit the shaping possibilities, but you can get an entire bowl (like the one shown in the top photo) from a single piece of 3/4"-thick stock. If you made the same bowl from solid wood, you'd need a 3"-thick blank that's 6" wide—not inexpensive in any wood.

Prepare the blank

There are numerous ways to glue up a blank for a segmented turning. You can bevel the ends of pieces at almost any angle to create a roughly circular shape—a pentagon, hexagon, or octagon. A stronger glue joint can be achieved with 45-degree mitered sections glued up as illustrated in the top drawing. Whichever method you choose, start by bevel-ripping the pieces to the desired angle (inset). Then apply a generous amount of glue

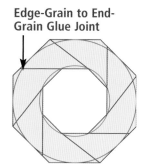

SEGMENT CUTTING OPTIONS

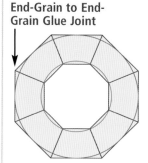

End-Grain to End-Grain Glue Joint

Edge-Grain to End-Grain Glue Joint

Method 1 creates thick walls.

Method 2 creates thinner walls but stronger glue joints.

to each cut edge and assemble the pieces into a ring. A band clamp is the best way to apply clamping pressure. If you want to recess a bottom as we did here, you'll also need to glue on a scrap block to the end of the blank, sandwiching a piece of kraft paper in between (bottom left photo).

Recess for the bottom

While the blank is drying, prepare a matching piece of wood for the bowl bottom. Cut an oversized blank and attach it to a faceplate with double-sided tape. Mount this on the lathe and true up the rim so it's perfectly square (inset photo). Remove this from the lathe, remove the bottom, and set it aside. When the glued-up blank has dried completely, attach a faceplate to the scrap block and mount the blank on the lathe. Then true up the end of the blank and cut a recess in the edge to fit the bottom you just trued up, as shown in the middle right photo.

Finish the bottom

When the bottom fits snug in the recess, remove it and apply glue to the recess. Then press the bottom in place and slide the tailstock over. Sandwich a round scrap between the tailstock center and the bottom of the bowl, and adjust the tailstock to press the bottom in place and serve as a clamp, as shown in the top left photo. After the glue has dried for an hour or so, remove the tailstock and scrap block and turn the bottom flat. Then turn a recess in the bottom to fit your scroll chuck, as shown in the top right inset photo.

Turn the exterior

Now you can turn the exterior of the bowl, as shown in the middle photo. Unless you used method 2 to glue up the blank, you won't encounter any end grain as you turn. This makes it easy to get a super-smooth exterior. When complete, remove the blank from the lathe, unscrew the faceplate, and use a chisel to separate the scrap block glued to the end. Then attach your scroll chuck to the headstock spindle and mount the blank onto the chuck to turn the interior.

Turn the interior

The simplest way to true up the inside face of the bowl is to cut into the edge with a heavy-duty square-nose scraper as shown in the bottom photo. You can also use a gouge; just make sure to take light cuts, particularly as you near the final wall thickness. Unlike a solid bowl blank, the walls of a segmented blank are only as strong as your glue joints. You can use a flat-nose scraper to touch up the bottom of the bowl as well. If all went well, sanding should be minimal.

GLUED-UP BLANKS

If you enjoy segmented turning (pages 94–95), you'll want to try another technique involving gluing up pieces of wood to form a blank. The possibilities are endless, and you can let your imagination run wild. The concept is simple: Glue up pieces of contrasting wood to create unusual designs. This can be as basic as sandwiching a layer of ⅛"-thick mahogany between quarter sections of maple as shown in the top photo to create an interesting platter, or slipping pieces of maple veneer between strips of walnut (see the platter on pages 186–189). The more elaborate the glue-up, the more visual impact you can achieve. Straight cuts, angled cuts, and varying thicknesses of wood can all be combined to make truly unique pieces.

Glue up the blank. Start by cutting your pieces to size. Then apply a generous amount of glue to each edge and glue up the blank as shown in the photo at right. Depending on the complexity of the blank, this could take several steps. For example, on the blank shown here, we started with a thin strip of mahogany and glued this between two strips of maple. After the glue dried, we cut the blank crosswise and then inserted another mahogany strip between the cut sections to form the cross design.

Mount the blank on the lathe. After you've allowed the glue to completely dry (we recommend overnight whenever possible), attach the blank to a faceplate or chuck. Then mount this onto the lathe, as shown in the photo at left (we used a faceplate ring to mount the blank onto our scroll chuck).

Turn the desired profile. Now you can turn the desired profile, as shown in the bottom right photo. Since a glued-up blank is generally not as strong as solid wood, take care when you initially present a turning tool to the blank. We've seen a number of glued-up blanks come apart on the lathe when a novice turner took too aggressive a cut. This is particularly possible if you've glued together end-grain sections, where the glue joint is not as strong as long-grain to long-grain.

Power-Sanding

Advanced turning often calls for advanced techniques to achieve the kind of finish you're after. That's because some shapes and woods are more difficult to cut smoothly and will require sanding. Conventional sanding often does not get the job done and it's best to turn to power-sanding. Power-sanding entails applying a spinning sanding pad to the rotating workpiece.

Removing stock quickly

If you need to remove stock quickly, your best bet is to use a rigid sanding disk like the one shown in the top photo. Because there's no padding, a rigid disk will quickly knock off imperfections. On the downside, you have to be really careful with how you present the disk to the workpiece to keep it from digging in and leaving grooves or swirl marks.

Sanding interiors

For general-purpose sanding and smoothing, go with a flexible disk or one that uses a pad,

like the New Wave disk (www.newabrasives.com) shown in the middle photo. Not only is the disk padded, but it also comes with an extra pad for handling tighter radii. This allows you to power-sand without sanding away details. Chuck the disk in your drill (we prefer to use a cordless drill so we don't have to wrestle with a cord) and attach the desired-grit sandpaper. Then turn on the lathe, then the drill, and ease the disk into the workpiece. Keep a firm grip on the drill, as the rotation of the workpiece can grab the drill and toss it about inside a bowl or platter. To prevent swirl marks, keep the drill moving as you sand. Switch grits as needed until the desired smoothness is achieved.

Sanding exteriors

You'll find that power-sanding the exterior of a bowl or other turning is much easier than the inside, as there's more room to move the sanding disk about, as shown in the bottom photo. Here again, you'll want to keep the drill moving and switch grits as needed to get a smooth finish.

Embellishing Turnings

As you progress in your turning skills, you'll eventually want to add a touch of distinction to your turnings. There are many, many ways to embellish turnings, and we'll describe just two of the more common ones: chatter marks and inlays. Chatter marks are made with a special turning accessory called a chatter tool. It's basically a stout handle with a hollow steel shank that accepts a thin pointed blade. When the thin blade makes contact with a spinning workpiece, it makes a small chip and then momentarily bends away from the workpiece, only to bend back and make another chip. Since the workpiece rotation is uniform and the blade bends or chatters at a uniform rate, a uniform design is cut into the surface. Although you can use a chatter tool on any wood or surface, it tends to leave the crispest design in the end grain of dense woods.

Chatter tool: Adjust the blade

Once you've mounted your workpiece on the lathe, the first step to using a chatter tool is to adjust the blade. The blade is held in place in the shank by either a setscrew or a threaded knob, as shown in the bottom left photo. Loosen the setscrew or knob and slide the blade in or out to the desired position. The more the blade extends, the more it will chatter and the greater the spacing between the chips. This really is one of the tools that you have to experiment with to find out what it can do.

Chatter tool: Position the tool rest

After you've adjusted the blade, you'll need to position the tool rest. What you're looking for here is to position the blade so it's slightly below the centerline of the blank, as shown in the top right photo.

Position the tool rest so that only the shank of the chatter tool sits on the tool rest, not the blade.

Chatter tool: Turn the design

With everything set up, turn on the lathe and press the blade tip into the workpiece as shown in the lower right photo. How much pressure you apply will determine how deep the chips are cut; more pressure means deeper chips. We recommend that you practice on a scrap of wood that's the same species as your workpiece to get the hang of this before cutting into your finished project.

Inlays are an excellent way to dress up a turning. You can use a contrasting inlay as shown here to create a dramatic effect. Or use a similar wood (like cherry inlaid into maple) for a more subtle look. Veteran turners can inlay almost anything into a turning, including turquoise, metal, and pearl or abalone. (For an example of an inlaid piece, see the project on pages 181–185.)

Inlays: Turn a groove

Once you've completed shaping and sanding your workpiece, you can lay out the groove for the inlay. Measure and mark carefully here, as too wide a groove could mean disaster. Cut the groove with a parting tool or a narrow square-nose scraper as shown in the top photo.

Inlays: Check the fit

Stop turning the groove when you near the marks you've made, and turn off the lathe. Then take a piece of your inlay and check the fit in the groove as shown in the middle photo. It's very important that you stop and check this frequently because it's very easy to cut a groove that's too wide. You'll want to cut the groove to a depth slightly less than the thickness of the inlay. This way after the inlay has been glued in place and dried, you can trim or sand it perfectly flush with the surface.

Inlays: Glue in the inlay

With the groove cut, you can cut your inlay to length to fit in the groove. This will take some patience, as it's best to cut the inlay long and slowly trim it to a perfect fit. Instead of butting the ends of the inlay strip together, we mitered the ends to create a scarf joint so the joint will be almost invisible. If you do this, you'll want to glue the inlay in the groove so that the top long miter of the joint faces the opposite the direction of the workpiece rotation. This will ensure that you won't catch the edge with a turning tool when you trim the inlay flush. The best tool to hold the inlay in place as it dries is a band clamp, like that shown in the bottom photo. Allow the glue to dry overnight before removing the clamp and finishing the piece.

5 Lathe Jigs and Fixtures

Most lathes are pretty much ready to go, out of the box. You can set the lathe on your bench, plug it in, and get to turning. There are, however, a couple of jigs and accessories you can build for your lathe that will make it more enjoyable and safer to use.

In this chapter, we'll show you how to build a tapered mandrel chuck for turning bracelets, etc.; a steady rest that will keep thin and long spindle work from flexing or bowing as you cut; a dust hood to keep that insidious sanding dust from coating your shop with a thin layer of sawdust; a nifty roll-around tool rack that not only keeps your lathe tools at your fingertips, but also stores all your lathe supplies and accessories; and a stout and rigid stand for your lathe.

Unlike most stationary power tools, a lathe does not require dozens of jigs and fixtures in order for you to realize its full potential. There are really only a couple of essentials, which include a tool rack and a lathe stand.

Tool Handles

Tool handles are easy to make on the lathe and can be custom-turned to fit your hands. They are an excellent way to use up those scraps of wood you just can't get yourself to throw away. We've provided patterns for three common handle types: file handle, chisel handle, and a handle for a turning tool; see the top left photo and the drawing at right. Note that although the profiles illustrated here are fairly classic shapes, they're just suggestions, and you can modify both the profile and length to suit the particular tool you have in mind for a handle.

As far as wood species is concerned, you'll find that tight-grained woods work best for smaller handles, as these have less of a tendency to split. Also, we recommend that you terminate the business end of each handle with a ferrule to prevent the handle from splitting as the tool tang is driven into the handle. The ferrules shown here are just lengths of copper pipe cut to length and then polished with a buffing pad.

TOOL HANDLE PATTERNS

Copper or Brass Ferrule

Chisel Handle

File Handle

Turning Tool Handle

Lay out the profile on the blank

To make a tool handle, first cut a blank to rough size and prepare the ends for spindle-turning (see pages 44–45), mount the blank on the lathe (page 46), and turn it to a rough cylinder (pages 50–51). Then use a rule or one of the patterns provided above right (or make up your own) to lay out the transition points on the blank with a pencil, as shown in the bottom right photo.

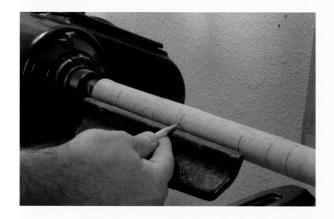

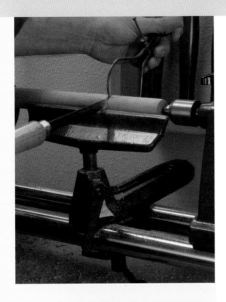

Define the profile

With the profile marked on the blank, use a parting tool and calipers to define the diameter at each of the points you marked on the blank, as shown in the top photo. Pay particular attention when sizing the tenon that the ferrule will slip over. You're after a slight friction-fit here. Use a set of inside calipers to measure the inside diameter of the pipe you're using, and transfer this measurement to a set of outside calipers to define the tenon.

Turn the profile

When you've got all the transition points defined

and the tenon is shaped, go ahead and turn the profile as shown in the middle photo. Stop periodically as you turn the profile, and grip the handle to see how it feels in your hand. Modify the profile as needed for a comfortable fit. Sand the completed profile and apply a finish if desired (see pages 74–75 for more on lathe-applied finishes).

Add the ferrule and tool

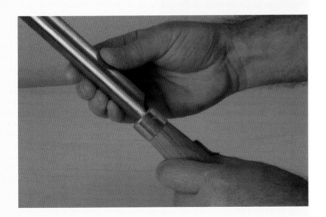

All that's left is to add the ferrule and tool. Depending on the tang of the tool, this will mean drilling either a single hole (for a round tang) or a series of holes to create a slot for a rectangular tang. Before you insert the tool tang, slip the ferrule over the tenon as shown in the bottom inset photo. No glue is needed here, as the tang will force the wood of the tenon to expand as it's driven in to lock the ferrule in place. Finally, fit the tang of the tool into the handle as shown in the bottom left photo. It should slip in only partway. Then you'll need to drive it the rest of the way in with a mallet and a scrap of wood to protect the tool's edge.

Tapered Mandrel Chuck

A tapered mandrel chuck like the one shown in the top photo and illustrated in the drawing below is a useful way to hold any workpiece for turning that has a space in its center (like a bracelet or a small round picture frame). Although you can make a tapered mandrel for a specific project, it's better to have one with a gradual taper to accept a wide range of workpieces.

Rough out the cylinder

To achieve a varied taper, you'll need to start with a fairly think blank. For the tapered mandrel shown here, we glued up three lengths of 2¥6 and then knocked off the corners to form an octagon to make truing up the cylinder easier. We used 12" lengths of 2¥6, but you could use almost any length that will fit between the centers of your lathe. Prepare the blank and mount it on the lathe. Then use a roughing gouge or spindle gouge to turn the blank into a rough cylinder as shown in the bottom photo.

MANDREL CHUCK DETAILS

12"

1"

3"

4½"

2½"

Drive Center

Live Center of Tailstack

END VIEW

Kerfs Cut for Drive Center

Hole Drilled for Live Center

END VIEW

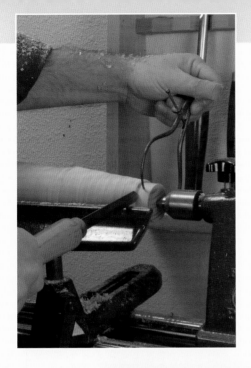

Define the taper

Once you've roughed out a cylinder, the next step is to define the taper with a parting tool and calipers, as shown in the top photo. One way to get a smooth taper is to first draw out the taper on scrap paper and measure the diameter at intervals of 1" or so and use these measurements to define the taper.

Rough out the taper

With the taper defined, go ahead and rough out the taper with either a roughing gouge or spindle gouge as shown in the middle photo. Stop frequently and check to see whether the taper is flat by laying a metal straightedge along the taper. Any highs or lows should be knocked off before moving to the next step.

Finish off with a skew

After the taper is roughed out, all that's left is to turn it smooth with a skew chisel as shown in the bottom photo. To use the tapered mandrel, back off the tailstock and slip the workpiece over the small end of the mandrel. Reposition the tailstock to hold the mandrel firmly in place and then slide the workpiece down the mandrel until it binds. If necessary, turn a small flat on the mandrel to better grip the workpiece. Before you turn the part, rotate the mandrel by hand to make sure the workpiece is on straight and doesn't wobble. Readjust its position as needed.

Steady Rest

If you've ever tried turning a long, thin spindle, only to have it bow and flex whenever you tried to make a cut, you understand the need for a steady rest. A steady rest is an accessory that attaches to your lathe bed. Most are semicircular, with three adjustable arms. The ends of the arms are tipped with rubber or plastic rollers. The arms are adjusted to contact the spindle in three places to keep the spindle from bowing under the cutting pressure of a turning tool. You can purchase a steady rest, but the shop-made version shown here will do the job just as well and can be built for little money.

Our steady rests consists of three main parts: a base that supports the holder, a holder that the arms attach to, and sliding arms that contact the work-piece; see the exploded view drawing on the opposite page. Each steady arm is slotted and attaches to the holder by way of a guide pin and a threaded stud that fits into a threaded insert in the holder. The guide pin keeps the arm from angling out of place once it's locked into position with the threaded stud. Inexpensive nylon rollers are mounted on the ends of the arms to keep from marking or damaging the workpiece.

Cut the holder to shape

To make the steady rest, start by laying out the holder pattern shown below on a piece of premium plywood such as Baltic Birch or Appleply. It's important to use a premium plywood here as these use many plies for excellent strength and are guaranteed to be gap-free. Make sure to locate and center-punch all holes for hardware. Then cut out the shape with a scroll saw (as shown in the photo at right), saber saw or band saw. Sand the edges smooth if necessary.

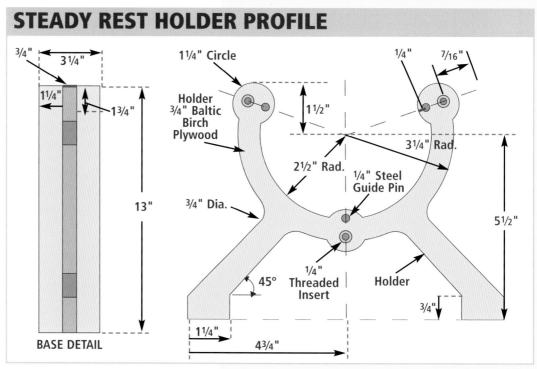

STEADY REST HOLDER PROFILE

BASE DETAIL

3/4" · 3 1/4" · 1 1/4" · 1 3/4" · 13"

1 1/4" Circle · Holder 3/4" Baltic Birch Plywood · 1 1/4" · 7/16" · 1 1/2" · 3 1/4" Rad. · 2 1/2" Rad. · 1/4" Steel Guide Pin · 3/4" Dia. · 5 1/2" · 45° · 1/4" Threaded Insert · Holder · 3/4" · 1 1/4" · 4 3/4"

Drill holes for the hardware

With the holder cut to shape and sanded, drill two sets of holes in the holder: one set for the threaded inserts and one set for the guide pins. If possible, drill these holes on the drill press to ensure that they are perpendicular to the face of the holder, as shown in the top left photo.

The guide pin holes are ¼" diameter, and the hole diameter for the threaded inserts should be drilled per the insert manufacturer's recommendations.

Install the holder hardware

Once the holes are drilled, go ahead and install the hardware in the holder. You can either cut ¼" metal rod to length or purchase precut pins at your local hardware store or home center. Use epoxy to secure these in the holes in the holder. How you install the threaded inserts will depend on whether they are screw-in or pound-in. We used the pound-in variety and tapped them in place with a hammer, as shown in the upper right photo.

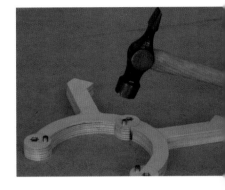

STEADY REST EXPLODED VIEW

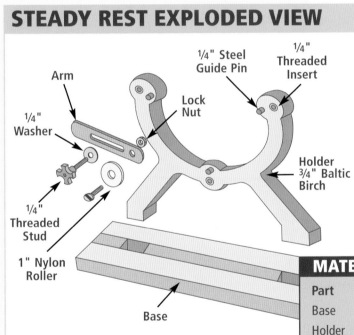

Arm

¼" Washer

¼" Threaded Stud

1" Nylon Roller

Base

¼" Steel Guide Pin

Lock Nut

¼" Threaded Insert

Holder ¾" Baltic Birch

MATERIALS LIST

Part	Quantity	Dimensions
Base	1	3¼" ¥ 13" – ¾"*
Holder	1	7" ¥ 9" – ¾" Baltic Birch
Arms	3	¾" ¥ 3½" – ¼" hardboard
Rollers	3	¼" ¥ 1" – nylon
Inserts	3	¼"
Studs	3	¼" threaded studs
Washers	6	¼"
Washers	6	10/32
Screws	3	10/32 ¥ ¾"
Guide pins	3	¼" steel rod, ¾" long

*Width is achieved by gluing up strips.

Glue up the base

Now that the holder is complete, you can turn your attention to the base. You could lay out and cut a square through mortise for the holder in a solid piece of wood, but we find it easier to build up the base from strips, leaving rectangular spaces for the legs of the holder. The outside strips are 1¼" wide and 13" long. The center pieces are all ³/4" wide, and the end pieces are 1³/4" long, with the center strip being 7" in length. Glue the strips together, taking care to leave the appropriate-sized holes for the holder, as shown in the top photo.

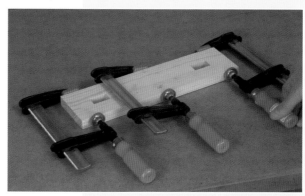

Glue the holder to the base

Once the base is dry, you can add the holder. Just spread some glue inside the open mortises and insert the holder as shown in the middle photo. While the glue dries, start work on the steady arms as described on the next page.

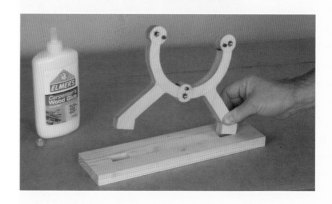

STEADY ARM PROFILE AND CROSS SECTION

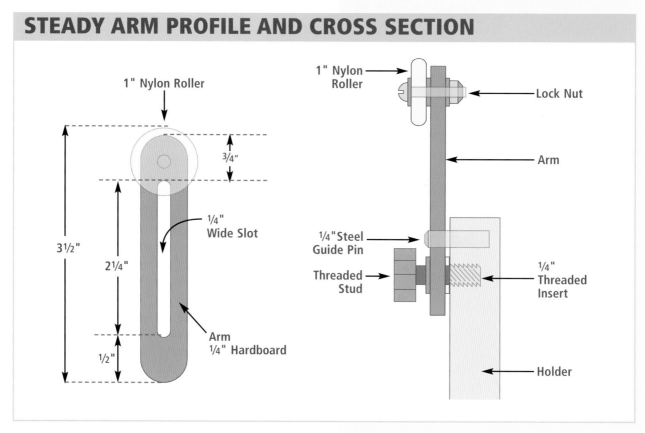

1" Nylon Roller

3/4"

3½"

2¼"

½"

¼" Wide Slot

Arm
¼" Hardboard

1" Nylon Roller

Lock Nut

Arm

¼" Steel Guide Pin

Threaded Stud

¼" Threaded Insert

Holder

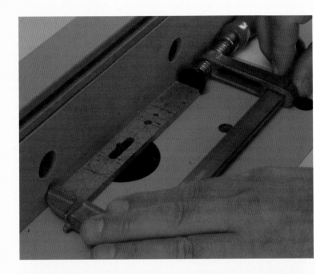

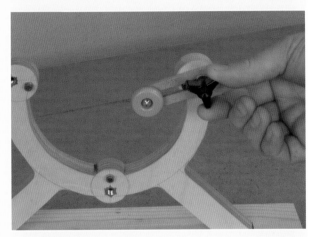

Create slots in the arms

All that's left is to make the steady arms and attach them to the holder. The arm itself is made from a strip of ¼" hardboard. To make it safer to rout the slots in these small arm pieces, cut them overlong and trim them to length after the slots have been routed. Once the strips are cut extra long, lay out the hole locations in each arm: two holes to define the beginning and end of the slot, and the hole near the end for the nylon roller; see the drawing on the bottom of page 108. Drill the holes on the drill press as shown in the top right photo. Then hold the strip between the jaws of a clamp as shown in the top left photo and rout the slot, using a ¼" straight bit. Alternatively, cut out the slot with a coping saw.

Add rollers and assemble

With the slots routed, trim the arms to length and round over the ends as shown in the arm profile drawing on the bottom of page 108. Attach a nylon roller to the end of each arm with 10/32 screws, washers, and nuts as shown in the middle right photo. When the arms are assembled, mount each to the holder by slipping the slot over the guide pin and threading in a threaded stud as shown in the middle left photo.

Using the steady rest

We didn't add a clamping mechanism to the rest shown here, as there are many different types and sizes of lathe beds. If you have a split bed, it's easy to make a simple clamp by installing a T-nut centered on the base to accept a bolt or threaded stud that passes through a cleat under the bed that spans the width of the bed. Alternatively, if your bed is flat, you can attach it with clamps. Center the steady rest on your spindle and adjust the arms so they just make contact with the spindle, and then lock them in place as shown in the bottom photo.

Dust Hood

The lathe is one of the toughest tools in the shop to tame the mess it makes. Unlike other stationary tools, where chip flow is generally in the same direction (such as a jointer or planer), shavings from a lathe can go in every direction, depending on the tool used, its position, and the size and shape of the workpiece. We have yet to see a dust hood capable of collecting the heavy shavings coming off a lathe at all angles. For us it's not the shavings that create the worst mess (this is easily swept or vacuumed up)—it's the dust. The fine dust caused from sanding on a lathe can quickly coat every surface in your shop.

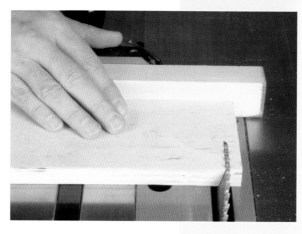

That's why we designed the articulated dust hood shown in the top left photo. It's fully adjustable to catch most sanding dust and is designed to work with your dust-collection system or shop vacuum. Please note that this hood will only be as good as your system. We hooked up our hood to our shop vacuum and noticed a huge difference in collecting ability when we replaced the old clogged filters with new, clean ones. Our dust hood consists of three main parts: a base with extension, a jointed arm, and a hood; see the exploded view on the opposite page.

Hood: Cut the back and sides

To make the dust hood, start by cutting the pieces to size as indicated by the materials list on the opposite page. The back and sides of the hood itself are angled to assist dust flow. Bevel-cut the ends of the hood back to a 15-degree angle on the table saw as shown in the middle photo. Then bevel-cut the ends of the hood sides as shown in the top right inset photo.

Hood: Drill the adapter hole

Next, drill a hole in the back of the hood to accept the adapter you'll use to connect to your dust-collection system or shop vacuum. Make sure to clamp the piece down securely as shown in the bottom photo. What you're after here is a tight friction-fit for the adapter. Cut the hole with a hole saw or an adjustable hole cutter.

DUST HOOD EXPLODED VIEW

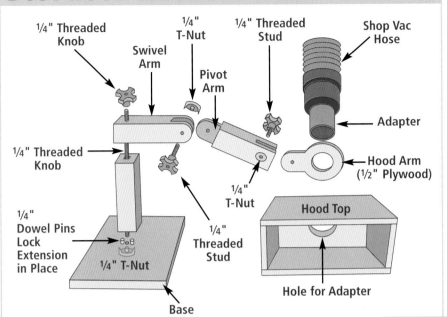

- 1/4" Threaded Knob
- Swivel Arm
- 1/4" T-Nut
- Pivot Arm
- 1/4" Threaded Stud
- Shop Vac Hose
- Adapter
- 1/4" Threaded Knob
- 1/4" T-Nut
- Hood Arm (1/2" Plywood)
- 1/4" Dowel Pins Lock Extension in Place
- 1/4" T-Nut
- 1/4" Threaded Stud
- Hood Top
- Hole for Adapter
- Base

Hood: Cut top/bottom and sides

The final hood parts are the top and bottom. The ends of these are also angled at 15 degrees to match the angled sides. Set the miter gauge on your saw for a 15-degree cut, and cut the ends of the top and bottom as shown in the photo above.

MATERIALS LIST

Part	Quantity	Dimensions
Hood back	1	3" ¥ 5 1/2" – 3/4"
Hood sides	2	3" ¥ 3 1/2" – 1/4" hardboard
Hood top/bottom	2	3 1/2" ¥ 7 1/2" – 1/4" hardboard
Base	1	6" ¥ 12" – 3/4" stock
Extension	1	1 1/2" ¥ 6" – 1 1/2"*
Swivel arm	1	1 1/2" ¥ 6" –1 1/2"
Pivot arm	1	1 1/2" ¥ 6" –1 1/2"
Hood arm	1	3" ¥ 4 1/2" – 1/2" plywood
Adapter	1	to fit your dust hose
Knob	1	1/4" threaded
Rod	1	1/4" threaded, 9" long
Threaded studs	2	1/4", 1 1/2" long
Dowel pins	2	1/4" ¥ 3/4" long
Lock nuts	3	1/4"
Washers	2	1/4"
Hose clamp	1	2"–3" clamp to fit your vacuum or dust collector hose

*Glued up from two 3/4"-thick pieces

DUST HOOD DETAILS

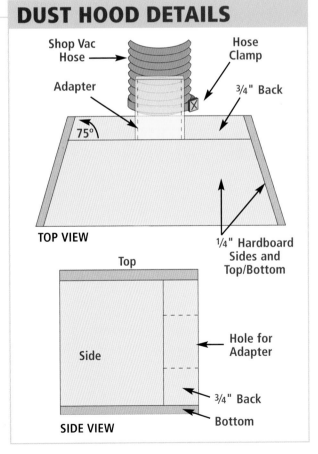

- Shop Vac Hose
- Hose Clamp
- Adapter
- 3/4" Back
- 75°
- 1/4" Hardboard Sides and Top/Bottom

TOP VIEW

- Top
- Side
- Hole for Adapter
- 3/4" Back
- Bottom

SIDE VIEW

Hood: Glue up hood

With all the hood parts cut to size, you can assemble the hood. Start by gluing the sides onto the angled ends of the back. When these are dry, glue on the top and bottom as shown in the top photo. Set this assembly to dry overnight, and begin work on the base and articulated arm.

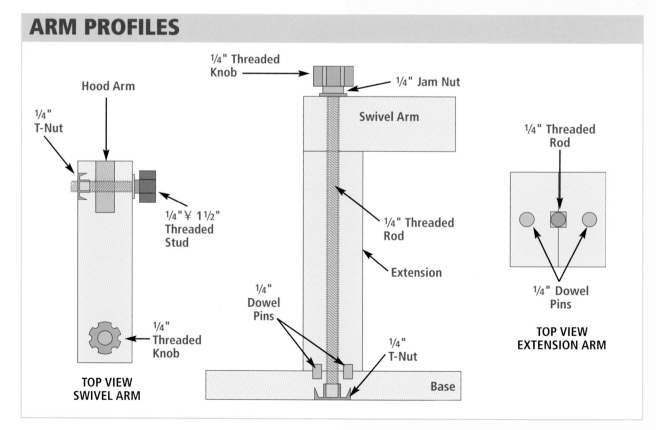

Base: Make the extension

The base of the dust hood consists of a two-piece extension and a base. A groove in the extension accepts a threaded rod that secures the articulated arm to the base, as shown in the exploded view on page 111. The rod threads into a T-nut mounted on the base. Instead of trying to drill a hole though the 6"

length of the extension, it's easier to create a hole by cutting centered grooves in two 3/4"-thick pieces and then gluing these together to form the 11/2" square extension. Cut matching 1/4"-wide by 1/8"-deep grooves in the extension halves (left inset photo) and glue them together as shown in the right photo below.

When the glue has dried, drill a pair of matching 1/4" holes in the bottom of the extension and base for a pair of dowel pins—these keep the extension from pivoting when the arm is adjusted. Then drill a hole for the T-nut and install it in the bottom of the base as shown in the drawing below.

ARM PROFILES

1/4" Threaded Knob

Hood Arm

1/4" T-Nut

1/4" Jam Nut

Swivel Arm

1/4" ¥ 11/2" Threaded Stud

1/4" Threaded Rod

Extension

1/4" Dowel Pins

1/4" T-Nut

1/4" Threaded Knob

TOP VIEW SWIVEL ARM

Base

1/4" Threaded Rod

1/4" Dowel Pins

TOP VIEW EXTENSION ARM

Arms: Mortise arms as needed

Now you can begin work on the articulated arm. Start by cutting the arm segments to length and then cut an open mortise in one end of the swivel arm and one end of the pivot arm. We did this with a tenoning jig on the table saw, fitted with a 1/2"-wide dado blade, as shown in the top photo. Cut these mortises 1 1/2" deep so they're centered on the thickness of the stock. Note: If you can't find 1 1/2"-thick stock, you can glue up each arm from two 3/4"-thick pieces.

Arms: Tenon arms as needed

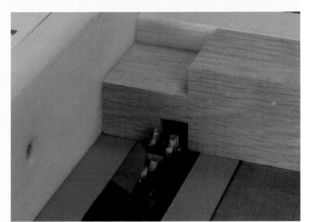

The next step is to cut a tenon on the end of the pivot arm opposite the open mortise, as shown in the pivot arm drawing on page 114. The tenon is 1 1/2" long and is sized to fit into the mortise on the swivel arm. We cut the tenon on the table saw, fitted with a dado blade, as shown in the middle photo. Start by cutting the tenon a bit fat, and then sneak up on the final fit by periodically testing it in the mortise in the swivel arm.

Arms: Round over ends as needed

In order for the pivot arm to pivot up and down freely in the mortise in the swivel arm, the ends of the mating parts must be rounded over—that is, the tenon end of the pivot arm and the mortise end of the swivel arm. Lay out a 1 1/2"-diameter arc on each end and cut the ends round with a scroll saw (as shown in the bottom photo), saber saw, or band saw. Then sand the rounded ends smooth. To complete the pivot and swivel arms, drill 1/4" holes as indicated for the threaded studs that clamp the parts together, as well as holes for the T-nuts that the threaded studs screw into; see the arm profiles on pages 112 and 114.

Arms: Drill hole in hood arm for adapter

The final arm part to make is the hood arm. This accepts the vacuum adapter and pivots up and down for optimum positioning of the hood. Lay out the shape on a piece of 1/2"-thick plywood (see the drawing below), and then drill a hole to fit your vacuum adapter, as shown in the top left photo. Then cut the hood arm to shape and sand the edges smooth.

Final assembly: Connect the arms

All that's left is to attach the arms to the base. Start by cutting a piece of threaded rod to length to pass through the extension and into the T-nut in the base. Allow enough so the top of the rod protrudes about 3/4" from the top of the swivel arm once it's in place. Then thread on a lock nut and a threaded knob or wing nut to the top of the rod to lock the swivel arm in place, as shown in the top right photo. Next, connect the pivot arm to the swivel arm and the hood arm to the pivot arm by screwing the threaded studs into the T-nuts in the arms, as shown in the inset photo at right.

PIVOT ARM AND HOOD ARM DETAILS

TOP VIEW

1/4" Hole

Pivot Arm

1/4" Threaded Stud

1/4" Washer

1/4" T-Nut

SIDE VIEW

1/4" Hole

Hood Arm
1/2" Baltic Birch

1/4" Hole

3/4" Rad.

1 1/4" Rad.

NOTE: Adjust radii of hood arm as needed to fit your adapter.

USING THE DUST HOOD

The dust hood is simple to use: Just clamp it in place, connect the hose, and adjust the arms for optimum dust collection.

Clamp the base to the lathe stand. To use the dust hood, first clamp the base to your lathe's stand or directly to the bed—whichever works better for you. Note that because the articulated arm swivels, you can orient the base so the front edge is parallel with your stand (as shown in the top photo) or perpendicular as needed for clamps to hold it in place.

Connect the dust hose. With the unit roughly in position, the next step is to connect your dust-collection hose to the arm. Note that we used a plastic adapter fitting to make the transition from a standard shop vacuum fitting to the smaller diameter needed for the hood. These adapters are available wherever shop vacuums are sold. If your lathe is up against a wall (as ours is), you may find it's easiest to attach a 90- or 45-degree plastic waste plumbing fitting to the end to navigate the tight curve, instead of bending your hose, which will tend to kink and restrict air flow, as shown in the middle photo. Also, for optimum suction, seal the connections with duct tape.

Adjust the arms and attach the hood

Finally, adjust the swivel, pivot, and hood arm as needed to lock the dust hood in the best position to collect dust. When in place, press the hood onto the adapter that protrudes from the hood arm as shown in the bottom photo. If the fit isn't tight enough to hold the hood in place, wrap a turn or two of masking tape around the end of the adapter and try again. Turn on your lathe and vacuum or dust collector and sand the part. Watch how the dust flows into the hood, and adjust as necessary for best collection.

Roll-Around Tool Rack

We've used a number of different styles of lathe tool racks over the years and have never been satisfied with any of them. Racks mounted on a wall behind the lathe require you to constantly reach over a spinning workpiece to grab a tool. To be safer, you could turn the lathe off—but doing this every time you change tools would add a lot of unnecessary time to your work (not to mention wear and tear on the lathe). Tool racks attached to the stand or in drawers are either in the way or just plain awkward to use.

What we wanted was a rack that put the tools right at our fingertips, regardless of whether we were turning between centers or doing faceplate or chuck work. This quickly led to the concept of a mobile or roll-around cart. While we were at it, we thought it'd be nice to have all our lathe accessories right at hand, so we added some drawers below the rack. The end result is the roll-around tool rack shown in the top left photo. The drawer units are modular, and you can add as many as needed below the rack to hold all your turning tools, accessories, and supplies. The roll-around rack consists of three main parts: a roll-around base, modular drawer assemblies, and an adjustable tilting rack to hold your tools; see the exploded view drawing on the opposite page.

Cut the base joinery

Start construction of the roll-around tool rack by making the mobile base. The base is made up of a pair of legs and vertical supports that are spanned by a bottom rail. The legs are joined to the vertical supports with half-laps; see the joinery detail below.

Begin by cutting centered notches on the legs, 3½" wide and 1½" deep, as shown in the top right photo. Then cut notches on the ends of the vertical supports to fit in the notches you cut in the legs, as shown in the middle inset photo. Miter-cut the ends of the legs and round over the tops of the vertical supports as shown in the drawing below.

BASE JOINERY DETAILS

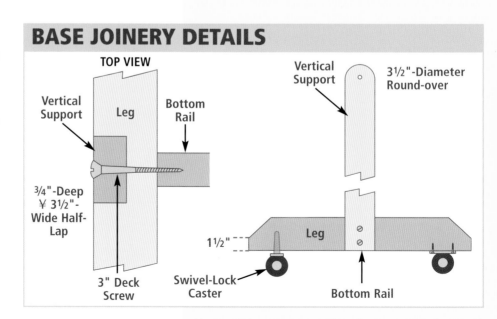

TOP VIEW

Vertical Support · Leg · Bottom Rail

¾"-Deep ¥ 3½"-Wide Half-Lap

3" Deck Screw

Vertical Support · 3½"-Diameter Round-over

1½"

Leg

Swivel-Lock Caster · Bottom Rail

Assemble the base

To assemble the base, start by gluing a vertical support into each leg. When the glue has dried, cut a bottom rail to length and then secure this between the base legs so it's centered on the legs and flush with the bottom of each leg. Use a clamp to temporarily hold the sides of the base in place so that you can drive screws through the base sides and into the bottom rail, as shown in the top left photo.

Install the casters

Remove the clamp and place the base on its side. Drill holes for the locking casters and snap them in place as shown in the top right photo. Alternatively, screw the mounting plates of the casters to the legs if the casters aren't the shank style shown here. Set the base aside and begin work on the drawer assemblies.

MATERIALS LIST

Part	Quantity	Dimensions
Legs	2	3½" ¥ 18" – 1½"
Vertical supports	2	3½" ¥ 36" – 1½"
Bottom rail	1	3½" ¥ 20⅛" – 1½"
Casters	4	2" locking swivel
Case sides	2	5" ¥ 14" – ¾" plywood
Center divider	1	4¼" ¥ 14" – ¾" plywood
Top/bottom	2	14" ¥ 19½" – ¾" plywood
Drawer sides	4	3½" ¥ 14" – ½" plywood
Drawer fronts/backs	4	3½" ¥ 8⅝" – ½" plywood
False fronts	2	4½" ¥ 9⅝" – ½" or ¾" stock
Knobs	2	1½"
Threaded studs	2	¼" ¥ 2" long
T-nuts	2	¼"
Drawer bottoms	2	8½" ¥ 13¼" – ¼" plywood
Rack sides	2	2½" ¥ 18" – ½" plywood
Rack top/bottom	2	2½" ¥ 19⅜" – ½" plywood
Rack back	1	17¾" ¥ 19¼" – ¼" plywood
Rack dividers	7	2" ¥ 17½" – ¼" plywood

TOOL RACK EXPLODED VIEW

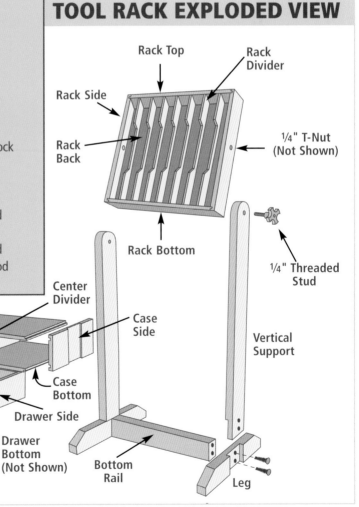

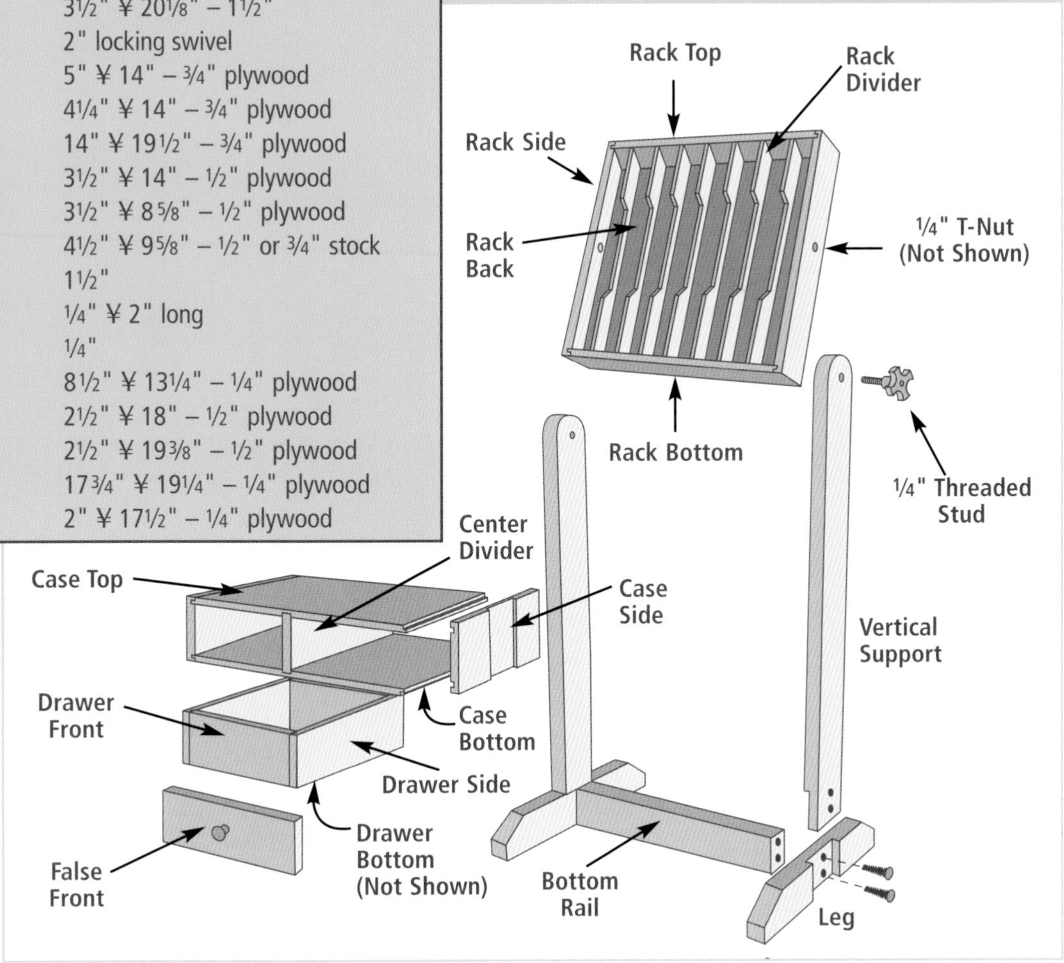

Rack Top

Rack Divider

Rack Side

¼" T-Nut (Not Shown)

Rack Back

¼" Threaded Stud

Rack Bottom

Center Divider

Case Side

Case Top

Case Bottom

Vertical Support

Drawer Front

Drawer Side

False Front

Drawer Bottom (Not Shown)

Bottom Rail

Leg

Cut case joinery

The sides and top and bottom of each drawer case are joined together with a tongue-and-groove joint, as illustrated in the drawing below. Start by cutting 1/4" by 1/4" grooves in the sides as shown in the top left photo.

Then cut tongues on the ends of the top and bottom to fit in the grooves as shown in the left inset photo . We used a table saw, fitted with a 1/4"-wide dado blade, for these cuts. Repeat these cuts for any additional drawer assemblies as desired.

Cut additional grooves

Next, cut a 1/4"-deep groove centered on the inside faces of the case top and bottom to accept the center divider. We used a 3/4"-wide dado blade in the table saw and set the rip fence to position the cut as shown in the top right photo. Then cut a 3 1/2"-wide shallow groove on the outside face of each side centered on its width, as shown in the right inset photo and the drawing below. This groove or notch fits over the vertical supports and serves to prevent the drawer units from racking over time.

CASE JOINERY DETAILS

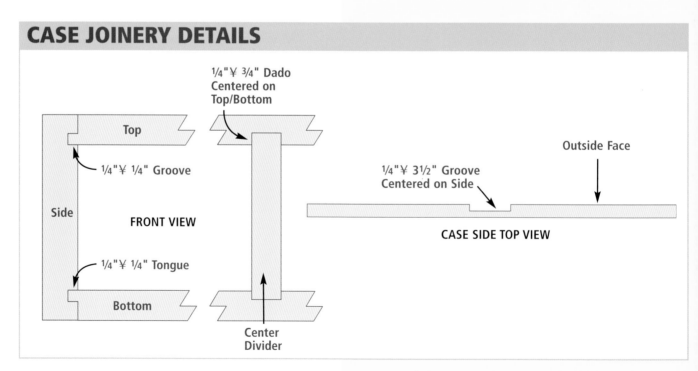

1/4"¥ 3/4" Dado Centered on Top/Bottom

Top

1/4"¥ 1/4" Groove

Side   FRONT VIEW

1/4"¥ 1/4" Tongue

Bottom

Center Divider

1/4"¥ 3 1/2" Groove Centered on Side

Outside Face

CASE SIDE TOP VIEW

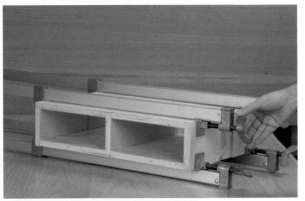

Assemble the drawer case

With all the case joinery complete, you can assemble the drawer case or cases. Start by applying glue to the tongues on the ends of the top and bottom as well as in the groove for the center divider. Place the center divider between the top and the bottom, and press the sides in place. Apply clamps as shown in the top photo, check for square by measuring the diagonals, and readjust the clamps and pressure as needed to square up the case. Allow the glue to dry overnight; repeat for any additional cases you have made.

Secure the case(s) to the base

When the glue on the case or cases has dried, go ahead and attach them to the base. Slip the case between the vertical supports so the groove in the sides fit over the supports, and position the top edge of the case 23" up from the bottom of the legs. We used clamps to temporarily hold the case in place while we drove in screws, as shown in the middle photo. You can either drive the screws through the supports into the case or through the case into the supports. If you do the latter, you'll need a right-angle drill fitted with a screwdriver bit or a stubby screwdriver to fit inside the case. Secure any additional drawer cases below the top one.

Cut the drawer joinery

Now you can turn your attention to the drawers. Just like the case, the drawer parts are joined with a tongue-and-groove joint, as illustrated in the drawing on page 120. Start by cutting 1/4" by 1/4" grooves in the drawer sides, and then cut tongues on the ends of the drawer fronts and backs to fit into these grooves as shown in the bottom photo.

Cut grooves for the drawer bottoms

When you've cut the tongue-and-groove joints, go ahead and cut a ¼" by ¼" groove in the inside bottom edge of each drawer piece to accept a ¼" plywood bottom, as shown in the top photo.

Assemble the drawers

That's it for drawer joinery—now you can assemble the drawers. Apply glue to the tongues on the ends of the front and back and in the grooves in each

piece for the bottom. Slip the back into one of the sides and insert the bottom. Then add the front and slip on the remaining side. Apply clamps as shown in the middle photo, check for square, and readjust as needed.

Install the drawers and add the false fronts

To complete the drawers, screw a false front onto each drawer so it's centered from top to bottom and from side to side, as shown in the bottom left photo. Insert the drawers to test the fit, and sand as needed to eliminate any binding. Finally, add a knob to each drawer.

DRAWER JOINERY DETAILS

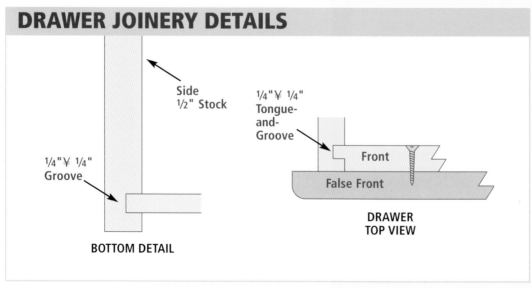

Side ½" Stock

¼" ¥ ¼" Tongue-and-Groove

¼" ¥ ¼" Groove

Front

False Front

BOTTOM DETAIL

DRAWER TOP VIEW

Cut the rack joinery

The final part to make is the tilting rack. It's basically an open box with dividers and is held in place with threaded studs that pass through the vertical supports and screw into T-nuts mounted on the inside faces of the rack sides. The rack also uses tongue-and-groove joints to join the sides and the top and bottom; see the drawing below. The dividers fit into 1/4" by 1/4" grooves cut in the top and bottom and are notched in the center to make it easier to lift out the tools. The rack back also fits into 1/4" by 1/4" grooves cut in each side and top and bottom. Cut the grooves and tongues as shown in the top photo and illustrated in the detail drawing below.

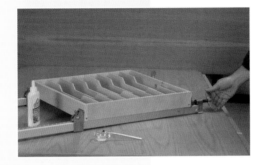

Assemble the rack

Apply glue to the tongues on the ends of the top and bottom and in the grooves for the back and dividers. Assemble the sides and top and bottom, slip in the dividers, and apply clamps as shown in the middle photo.

Attach the rack to the base

Drill a hole centered from end to end and across the width of each case side for a T-nut. Press the T-nut in place and then drill a hole centered on the top radius of each vertical support. Slip the rack between the vertical supports, and screw a threaded stud through each vertical support and into the T-nuts in the rack. Adjust the rack for a comfortable angle and lock it in place by tightening the threaded studs.

PIVOTING RACK DETAIL

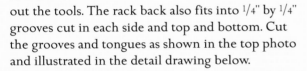

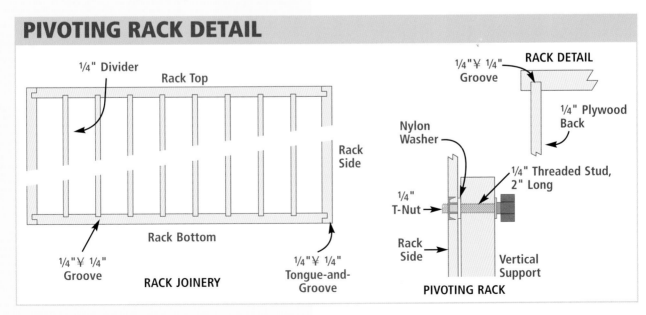

1/4" Divider

Rack Top

Rack Side

RACK DETAIL

1/4"¥ 1/4" Groove

1/4" Plywood Back

Nylon Washer

1/4" Threaded Stud, 2" Long

1/4" T-Nut

Rack Side

Vertical Support

PIVOTING RACK

1/4"¥ 1/4" Groove

Rack Bottom

1/4"¥ 1/4" Tongue-and-Groove

RACK JOINERY

Lathe Stand

Vibration is the nemesis of a turner. To get smooth, clean cuts, the workpiece must be rotated with minimal vibration. A quality lathe will do a lot to hold down vibration, but much will depend on the stand that it's mounted on. A good lathe stand will be both heavy and rigid to help dampen vibration. The shop-built stand shown here is both—and it's inexpensive and easy to build. The bulk of the stand is made from MDF (medium-density fiberboard) which by itself is quite heavy—around 100 pounds per sheet. The top and sides are made of double layers of 3/4"-thick MDF and are held together with dovetail joints that will stand up to vibration and hold parts in place over time. A tray near the bottom of the stand can be filled with bricks or sand to add even more weight. Alternatively, you could hinge the tray lid and use this space for storing your tools and accessories.

Our lathe stand consists of two double-layer MDF sides that are spanned by front and back and top rails—all joined with single dovetails. The front and back rails form the front and back of the weight tray. A double-layer MDF top is edge-banded with solid wood to prevent dings and dents, and attaches to the top rails as illustrated in the

exploded view drawing on the opposite page.

Cut grooves in the sides
To make the stand as rigid as possible, the front and back rails are pulled into the sides via threaded rods that run though the width of each side. The simplest way to do this is to cut shallow matching grooves on the inside face of each side piece and then glue them together to create a groove for the rod. We cut the 3/8"-wide grooves on the table saw fitted with a dado blade, as shown in the middle photo.

Glue up the sides
Once you've cut the grooves in the sides, you can assemble each side assembly by gluing the pieces together with the grooves facing in. We applied a generous uniform coat of glue on the inside face of one side (taking care to stay about 1/2" away from the grooves) and placed this on the mating side piece so the edges aligned, and then screwed the pieces together with 1 1/4"-long screws as shown in the bottom photo. With the side pieces joined, lay out and cut the arcs on the bottom edges to create feet, as illustrated in the detail drawing on the opposite page.

LATHE STAND DETAILS

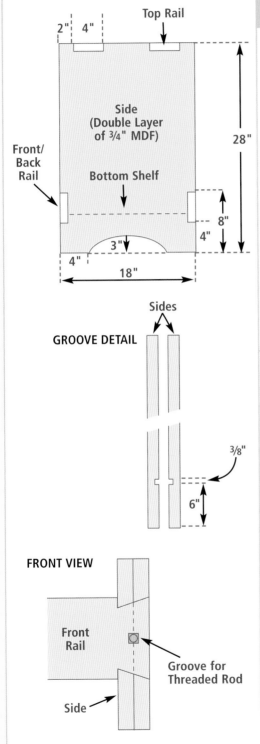

Top Rail

2" 4"

Side
(Double Layer
of 3/4" MDF)

28"

Front/
Back
Rail

Bottom Shelf

8"

4"

3"

4"

18"

Sides

GROOVE DETAIL

3/8"

6"

FRONT VIEW

Front
Rail

Groove for
Threaded Rod

Side

LATHE STAND EXPLODED VIEW

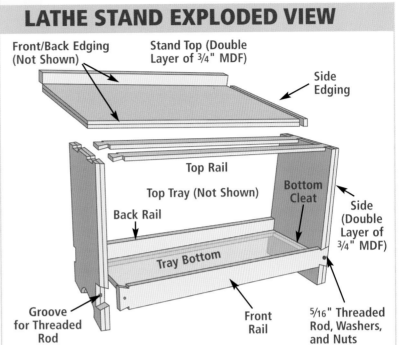

Front/Back Edging
(Not Shown)

Stand Top (Double
Layer of 3/4" MDF)

Side
Edging

Top Rail

Top Tray (Not Shown)

Bottom
Cleat

Back Rail

Side
(Double
Layer of
3/4" MDF)

Tray Bottom

Groove
for Threaded
Rod

Front
Rail

5/16" Threaded
Rod, Washers,
and Nuts

MATERIALS LIST

Part	Quantity	Dimensions
Sides	2	18" ¥ 28" – 1½" MDF*
Top rails	2	4" ¥ 42" – 3/4" stock
Front/back rails	2	4" ¥ 42" – 3/4" stock
Bottom side cleats	2	3/4" ¥ 15" – 3/4" stock
Bottom front/back cleats	2	3/4" ¥ 37½" – 3/4" stock
Tray bottom	1	16½" ¥ 39" – 3/4" MDF†
Tray top	1	18" ¥ 39" – 3/4" MDF†
Stand top	1	20" ¥ 44" – 1½" MDF*
Front/back edging	2	1½" ¥ 20" – 3/4" stock
Side edging	2	1½" ¥ 45½" – 3/4" stock
Threaded rods	2	5/16" ¥ 19" long
Washers	4	5/16"
Nuts	4	5/16"

*Two 3/4"-thick pieces glued together

†Cut to fit

DOVETAIL-ROUTING JIG

All of the single dovetail rails of the stand fit into dovetail-shaped recesses cut into the sides and tops of the stand sides. There are a number of ways you can create these recesses, but the simplest way to create uniform recesses is to use a shop-made jig for your router, as illustrated in the bottom drawing. The jig is just a pair of angled guides attached to a base and spanned in the rear by a cleat; it's designed to work with a standard ⅝" router bushing set and a ½" straight bit.

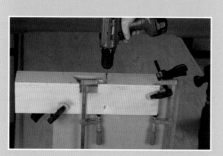

Lay out the dovetail. To make the jig, start by laying out the dovetails on the sides as shown in the top left photo and illustrated in the detail drawing on page 123 and in the drawing below.

Install bushing set. Next, install the bushing set in your router and insert a ½" straight bit. Adjust the bit so that it will cut a ¾"-deep notch when placed on top of the guides, as shown in the photo at right.

Assemble the jig. An easy way to assemble the jig is to clamp the base to a side and then locate the angled guides the appropriate distance away from the dovetail lines you marked on the side. For a ⅝" bushing, this means the guides should be 1/16" away from the outside of the lines. Clamp each guide in place and then screw it to the base as shown in the bottom left photo. Then cut a cleat to length and screw it to the back of the guides to add rigidity and create a stable platform for the router.

DOVETAIL AND JIG DETAILS

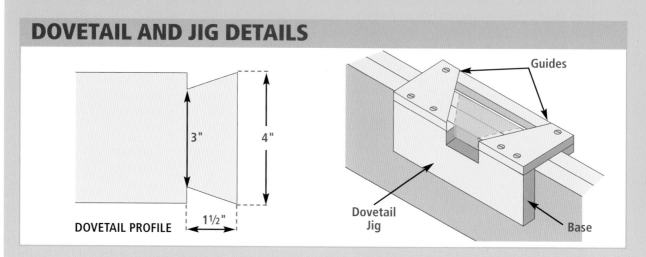

DOVETAIL PROFILE — 3", 4", 1½"

Guides

Dovetail Jig

Base

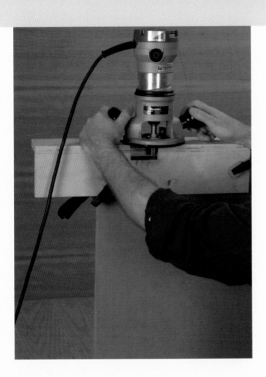

Rout dovetail notches in the sides

To use the dovetail-routing jig, temporarily clamp the jig to a side assembly so the guides are centered on one set of lines you marked earlier on the side. Then place the router on the jig and turn it on. Press the bushing up against one of the angled sides and begin the cut, taking care to keep the bushing in solid contact with the guide. As there's a lot of material to remove here, take your time and take light passes until the recess is formed, as shown in the top photo. Repeat for the remaining recesses.

Cut dovetails on the ends of the rails

Once the dovetail recesses have been routed in the sides, you can cut the "pins" on the ends of all four rails: the front and back rail and top rails. Lay these out per the drawing on page 124, and remove the waste with a hand-saw (as shown in the middle photo) or with a band saw, scroll saw, or saber saw. Use a sharp chisel to clean up the edges as needed.

Drill rod holes in the rails

Next locate the holes in the ends of the front and back rails for the threaded rods to pass through. These are centered on each pin from top to bottom and across the width of the pin. Once you've marked and center-punched the locations, drill the holes as shown in the bottom photo or at the drill press.

Attach the front/back rails to the sides

Now you're ready to start assembling the stand. Begin by slipping one end of the back rail in one side of the stand. Then slip the opposite end into the other side. Repeat this for the front rail. If the fit is snug, use a rubber mallet or dead-blow hammer to tap it in place as shown in the top right photo.

Secure the rails

At this point you should be able to slide the threaded rods through the holes in the front or back rails, through the sides, and back out a front or back rail. Slip a washer on each end of the threaded rod and thread on nuts. Tighten the nuts simultaneously with a pair of wrenches as shown in the middle photo to pull the rails tight into the sides.

Add the top rails

The top rails should fit cleanly in the recesses you routed in the tops of the sides. Set each top rail in place and secure each by driving $2^{1}/_{2}$" screws through the rails and into the sides, as shown in the bottom photo. ShopTip: Make sure to drill pilot holes for these screws first, as MDF tends to split if you just drive screws into the edge. Note that we didn't use glue to attach any of the rails; not only is it unnecessary because of the fasteners you're using, but no glue means you can disassemble the stand if you ever need to move it.

Attach cleats to the rails

With all the rails in place, the stand should be nice and rigid. As we mentioned earlier, the front and back rails form the front and back of the weight tray. The bottom of the tray is supported by cleats attached to the bottom inside edge of the rails and to the sides. Cut the cleats to fit and attach them with glue and screws, as shown in the top photo. Then cut cleats to fit between these, and attach them to the sides with glue and screws so their bottom edges are flush with the bottom edges of the front and back rail cleats.

Add the tray bottom

Now you can cut a bottom to fit inside the tray. This can be a single piece or two pieces as shown in the middle photo. No glue or fasteners should be needed here, since the weight of the bricks, sand, or tools and accessories will hold the bottom in place.

Glue up the top

The next step is to make the top. Start by cutting two pieces of 3/4"-thick MDF to size. Then apply a generous coat of glue to one inside face and press on the other piece. Align the edges and screw the pieces together with 1 1/4"-long screws as shown in the bottom photo.

Add the edging

We edged our MDF top with solid wood to help protect the edges of the MDF. Solid wood will stand up better to dings and dents versus MDF, which will tend to chip. We joined the edging to the MDF top with biscuits (as shown in the top photo), but you could use dowels or simply screw the edging in place. Whichever fastening method you choose, make sure to apply a generous coat of glue to the edges of the top before clamping the edging in place (inset photo).

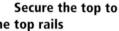

Secure the top to the top rails

After the glue has dried on the edging, remove the clamps and position the top on the stand. Center it from side to side and from front to back. Then secure it to the stand by driving 2"-long screws up through the top rails and into the underside of the top, as shown in the middle photo.

Position the stand

The stand is almost complete now, so now's the time to move it to its intended destination. Even without the added weight of the sand or bricks and the lathe, it's already heavy. Make sure you get a helper to lift the stand in place, as shown in the bottom photo.

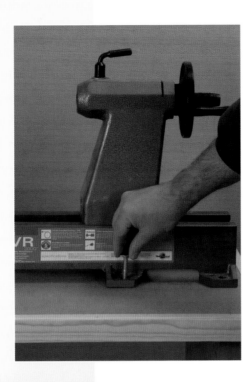

Mount the lathe

With the stand located where you want it, you can mount your lathe to it. Here again, get a helper to assist you in moving the lathe and place it on top of the stand. In most cases, you'll want to center it from front to back and from side to side, but you may choose to position it differently. When you've determined the exact location, drill holes through the mounting holes in your lathe, through the double-layer top, and attach the lathe to the stand with nuts and bolts as shown in the top photo.

Add weight to the bottom tray

At this point you'll have to decide whether to use the tray for additional weight or for storage. Either way, add whatever contents you have in mind to the tray, as shown in the middle photo. Bricks are easy to load in for extra weight, but they're not as heavy as sand. The only thing to keep in mind when using sand is to make sure it's dry before pouring it into the tray. Most sand available at home and garden centers is stored outside and is usually wet. If you put this in the tray without it being totally dry, excess moisture will wick into the rails and MDF sides. And MDF will suck up water and expand just like particleboard will—like a sponge.

Add the tray top

All that's left is to add the tray top as shown in the bottom photo. If you used the tray to add weight to the stand, just fasten the top with a couple of screws. If you're planning on using the tray for tool storage, attach the lid to the back rail with hinges for easy access.

6 Maintenance and Troubleshooting

A quality lathe costs a lot of money. Protect your investment by maintaining your lathe on a regular basis. In addition to protecting your investment, routine maintenance will also keep the lathe running smoothly and safely and will also help prevent small problems from developing into a major breakdown.

In this chapter we'll show you how to inspect, clean, and lubricate your lathe. Then we'll cover some basic repairs and ways to eliminate the often troublesome vibration. The remainder of the chapter delves into keeping lathe tools in peak condition. Basic and modified profiles are discussed, along with step-by-step directions on how to grind freehand, using jigs and using a water-cooled system. Finally, we'll cover manual and power honing so that you can keep your lathe tools razor-sharp.

The tools and supplies needed to keep your lathe running in tip-top condition are few and inexpensive; equipment for sharpening lathe tools, on the other hand, can be costly but are well worth the investment.

Inspection

Like any other power tool, a lathe should be periodically inspected to keep it running in tip-top condition and to identify any problems early on so they don't develop into major headaches later.

In particular you should routinely check the headstock spindle for run-out, and check the motor and its V-belts and the lathe bed and stand.

Run-out

For a lathe to run smoothly and vibration-free, the headstock spindle must be perfectly straight. If it's bent even slightly or machined improperly, the spindle will wobble and cause the workpiece to vibrate. Run-out is the technical term for how true the spindle is, and it's identified by the amount of deviation the spindle is off center. The most accurate way to test a headstock spindle for run-out is with a dial indicator, like the one shown in the photo at left. To use a dial indicator, clamp it to your lathe bed and adjust the probe so it just makes contact with the spindle. Zero the dial and then manually rotate the spindle by turning the handwheel. Watch the dial: Any run-out will cause a deflection on the dial. Any more than a couple thousandths of an inch and you should contact the manufacturer.

Simple run-out test

If you don't have a dial indicator on hand, you can do a quick and inexpensive test by clamping a square block of wood so it almost touches the spindle, as shown in the upper right photo. Then rotate the spindle by turning the handwheel as you watch the gap for variations between the block and the spindle.

If you note any, use a feeler gauge to identify the gap and consult the manufacturer of your lathe if it's more than a couple thousandths of an inch.

Motor

Your motor should be inspected frequently, particularly if you use the lathe a lot. Check the cord for fraying and replace it if necessary (see page 138). It's also a good idea to routinely remove the fan cover to inspect the cooling fins of the fan, as shown in the bottom photo. Bent or missing fins can lead to vibration and should be repaired or replaced as needed. While you're in there, blow out any dust and debris with a blast of compressed air.

V-belts

If your lathe is belt-driven, check the belt occasionally for excessive wear and tear; replace it if necessary. At the same time, it's a good idea to clean the pulleys. Many belt-driven lathes use grooved pulleys to engage a grooved belt. With use, the grooves can fill with dirt, dust, and debris. These can be easily cleaned with an old toothbrush, as shown in the top photo, or with a brass brush.

Bed

The bed of your lathe is somewhat similar to the table of a table saw—it's one of the hardest-working surfaces of the tools. The tool rest and tailstock are constantly being slid across the bed and then locked in place. Inspect the bed of your lathe every time you start a turning project. It only takes a second to make sure all is well. Pay particular attention to the area adjacent to  the headstock, as this is where excess finish often ends up if you finish your projects on the lathe. If you find any finish residue, scrape it off with a putty knife as shown in the middle photo.

Stand

The lathe stand is often the most overlooked part of a lathe when it comes to inspection, since it's easily taken for granted. But as we've mentioned previously, the condition of the stand plays a big part in the overall performance of the lathe. Regardless of whether the stand is bolted-together metal (as shown in the bottom photo) or shop-made, check to make sure that all fasteners are tight and that the stand is rigid. Try giving it a shove from a couple different directions—it shouldn't budge. If it does, tighten hardware or repair the stand as needed.

Cleaning

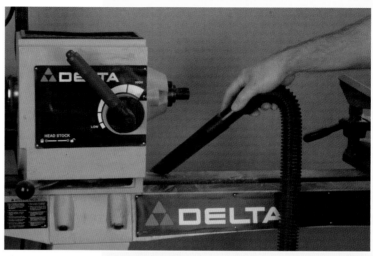

As a general rule of thumb, a lathe should be cleaned after every use to keep dust and shavings from building up and causing problems. In addition to this, the headstock spindle and the lathe bed need special attention, as described below.

Vacuum

A clean lathe is a happy lathe—no, really. The cleaner the moving parts on a lathe are—like the tool rest and tailstock—the better it can perform. After every job, pull out the shop vacuum and whisk away dust and shavings, as shown in the top photo. If you turn green wood, pay particular attention to any spaces or gaps in the bed where wet shavings can accumulate and cause the bed to rust.

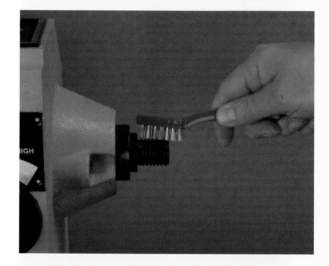

Brass brush for threads

The headstock spindle gets a lot of use, so it needs to be cleaned regularly. We've found that a brass brush (like the one shown in the middle photo) works best to ferret out built-up grease and dust that's easily trapped in the spindle threads. It's also a good idea to clean inside the Morse taper occasionally. Although you can buy a special "reaming" tool for this, a circular brass brush (like those used to clean guns) works just as well.

Abrasive pad for the bed

The smoother and cleaner the lathe bed, the easier you'll be able to slide the tool rest base and tailstock around. We like to scrub the lathe bed occasionally with a nonabrasive pad wrapped around a scrap block to keep it flat, as shown in the bottom photo. The idea here is just to get any surface impurities off, along with any finish residue.

Lubrication

Along with regular inspection and cleaning, various parts of the lathe should be routinely lubricated as illustrated in the drawing at the bottom of page 136.

Dead centers

The type of centers you use on your lathe will determine whether they need to be lubricated or not. The heads or tips of most centers do not require lubrication. But if you use a cup or "dead" center, apply a dollop of white lithium grease to the end as shown in the top photo. This lubricant will help the workpiece spin in the cup without burning.

Morse tapers

The tapered portion of all centers can use some periodic lubrication. Before you apply any, take the time to scrub the surface gently with a non-abrasive pad to remove any goo or rust built up on the surface. Then spray on a very light coat of dry lubricant as shown in the middle photo. Do not use machine oil, since this will only cause the center to spin inside the Morse taper. A dry lubricant will make it easier to remove the center without causing it to spin inadvertently.

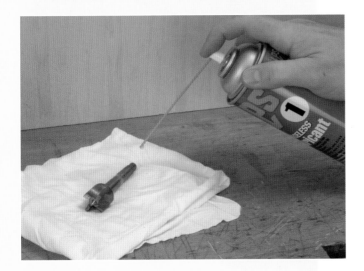

Chucks

As with a Morse taper, it's best to clean a lathe chuck thoroughly before applying a lubricant. Most can be cleaned with compressed air or by wiping the chuck with a clean, dry cloth. Most chuck manufacturers suggest applying a lubricant to the back of the accessory jaws before mounting them on the jaw slides (bottom photo). This helps prevent the jaws from "freezing" in place on the slides. Just wipe on a thin coat of light machine oil. Consult the chuck owner's manual to see whether they suggest a specific lubricant and whether you should oil any other parts.

Headstock

The type of bearings that support the spindle in your headstock will define whether they need lubrication or not. Most use sealed bearings that don't require—and don't allow—periodic lubrication. Some lathes, like the Record CL48 shown in the top left photo, use bronze bearings that require a drop or two of light machine oil periodically.

Tailstock

The shaft of a tailstock moves in and out as the center is adjusted and needs a coat of light machine oil every now and then, as shown in the top right photo. First extend the tailstock out. Then apply a light coat of oil and immediately wipe off any excess to keep dust from attaching to the oil and forming a thick goo. Alternatively, consider spraying the tailstock shaft with a dry lubricant—this way you won't have to worry about dust forming into goo.

LATHE LUBRICATION POINTS

Drive Center
(Light Machine Oil)

Tailstock Center and Position Locks
(Light Machine Oil)

Motor Pulleys
(White Lithium Grease)

Bed
(Paste Wax)

Tailstock Handle
(Light Machine Oil)

Tool Rest, Locking Levers
(Light Machine Oil)

Swivel Lock or Speed Control
(Light Machine Oil)

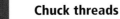

Spindle

As you're likely to be constantly screwing lathe accessories on and off the headstock spindle, it should be lubricated frequently. Consult your owner's manual for a recommended lubricant. We've found that a light application of white lithium grease does an adequate job for most lathes. Just squirt a dollop onto the threads (as shown in the top photo) and work the grease into the threads with a soft, clean cloth.

Chuck threads

Some chuck manufacturers also recommend that you apply a light coat of grease to the inside threads of the chuck that screws onto the head-stock spindle, as shown in the middle photo. Here again, white lithium grease works well and it is best applied with a cotton swab.

Bed

Finally, to keep everything sliding smoothly on the bed of the lathe, spray on a dry lubricant and then wipe off any residue, as shown in the bottom photo. Alternatively, you can apply a coat of paste wax. If you turn frequently, this can be done as often as once or twice a week. We think you'll be pleasantly surprised to find how much easier things slide on a well-lubricated lathe bed.

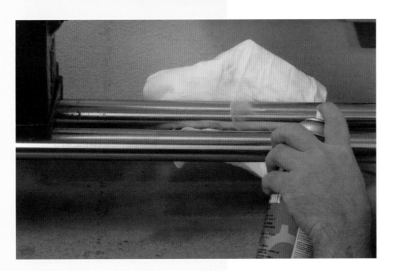

Lathe Repair

If you inspect your lathe frequently (pages 132–133), you just might catch a problem before it gets serious. This way you can purchase a repair part well in advance of a breakdown to allow you to replace the part at your leisure. In a perfect world, this is how it happens. Unfortunately, not all breakdowns can be ferreted out via regular inspections. Sometimes a part just fails and needs replacing. The most common lathe parts to fail are related to the motor: the power switch and cord and the belts and pulleys. But a part doesn't have to fail to cause problems. Frequently you'll notice a bit more vibration, and we'll show you the common causes of this plus ways to eliminate it (see pages 140–141).

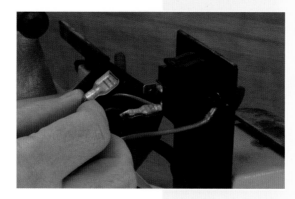

Replacing a power switch

Of all the electrical components on a lathe, the power switch is the most likely to fail over time because of its constant use. Fortunately, replacing a power switch on most lathes is simple. Start by ordering a replacement switch. When it arrives, unplug your lathe and remove the switch box cover or access panel. Then remove the switch from the housing by unscrewing the mounting screws or popping the plastic clips that hold it in place, as shown in the top photo. The foolproof way to replace it is to remove one wire at a time off the old switch and attach this wire to the new switch. Once the wiring has been transferred to the new switch, remount it in the box and replace the cover or access panel. Plug in the lathe and test it.

A new electrical cord

The next likely electrical part to fail is the power cord—especially if it runs along a floor where it can get stepped on. If your power cord is damaged or frayed, replace it. Spare cords can be found at most hardware stores and home centers for emergencies; but you'll be better off ordering an exact replacement cord, as this will ensure that it's the proper length and gauge for your motor. Also, the individual wires are usually terminated with the appropriate screw or push-tab terminals, as shown in the middle photo. Just as you would with a power switch, remove a wire from the old cord and connect the matching wire on the new cord. Repeat for all wires, remount the cord cover or panel, and test.

Replacing a motor

If the windings in your motor short or open, you'll need to replace the motor. Although some motors can be rewound, by the time you pay for this, you may as well order a new motor. The motors on lathes that are belt-driven are simple to replace. Start by unplugging the lathe, loosening the belt tension, and removing the belt. Then loosen the motor-mounting bolts as shown in the bottom photo. Disconnect wiring one wire at a time and connect these wires to your new motor. Repeat for all wires and mount the new motor, slip on the belt, and adjust belt tension. Plug in the lathe and test.

Replacing a drive belt

Inside the motor housing, the belt is the most likely part to fail, as it's under constant tension and is relied on to drive the headstock spindle. Belts that are frayed, are cracked, or show excessive wear should be replaced (top left photo).

Although you might think replacing a belt is simple, it often isn't because the pulley that connects to the headstock spindle rotates on a continuous shaft. But most belt-driven lathes have a handwheel shank that connects to the headstock spindle. This setup allows you to loosen the screws that hold the handwheel shank onto the spindle so you can slide it out to create a gap for slipping off the belt; consult your owner's manual for the recommended procedure.

A new pulley

The step pulleys inside the motor housing rarely need replacing, as they are well protected from dirt and debris and are made of either aluminum, machined steel, or cast iron. Occasionally, a pulley can get damaged—usually from debris getting inside the motor housing—and needs to be replaced. The step pulley that connects to the motor spindle is as easy to replace as loosening a setscrew, sliding off the old pulley, and installing the replacement pulley, as shown in the top right photo. The pulley that rides on the headstock spindle usually requires removing the handwheel and possibly the headstock spindle; consult your owner's manual to see what the recommended procedure is or whether you should have this done professionally.

REPLACING BEARINGS

Although relatively rare for the average woodturner, lathe bearings—those that support the headstock spindle—can fail, especially when large or heavy objects are frequently turned. Heavy loads can exert tremendous lateral pressure on the bearings, causing them to wear excessively—typically they'll wear out of round. The one nice thing about bearings going bad is that it's pretty easy to identify the problem by the grinding or clicking noise you hear when the lathe is turned on or even when the spindle is rotated by hand. Also, the spindle should spin freely—no hang-ups or catches. If you feel any of these, the bearings are shot.

Should you replace the bearings yourself? Not unless you're a machinist and are capable of adjusting and tweaking a spindle for zero runout. And that's assuming you have bearing pullers on hand, know how to use them, and can get identical replacement bearings. You'll be better off having the bearing replaced professionally. If your lathe is heavy (and most are), check with your local tool service center or lathe manufacturer to see whether they do house calls. Yes, this will cost you, but it's a lot more convenient than trying to drag your lathe into the shop.

Minimizing Vibration

Any vibration generated or caused by the lathe will end up transferring to your workpiece. The result is less-than-smooth cuts, chatter, and even the occasional catch. If you are experiencing vibration, try one or more of the various techniques shown here to minimize it.

Level the lathe

The first thing you should do is to make sure your lathe is level. Place a torpedo or 3-foot level on the bed of the lathe to check for level, as shown in the top photo. If the bubble is off, adjust the legs of your stand, if they're adjustable, until it's level. (Note: You may need to loosen hardware on metal stands to friction-tight before doing this.) For stands without adjustable legs, add shims as needed.

Tighten the stand hardware

Once you're sure the lathe is level, check to make sure that the lathe is firmly attached to the stand and that the stand is rigid. Try bumping the edge with your hip in a couple of places. The stand should not shift. If the stand is metal (like the one shown in the middle photo), check all of the assembly nuts and bolts to make sure they're tight. Tighten any loose ones and add lock washers if necessary. For non-metal stands, replace, repair, or add parts as needed to shore up the stand.

Add more weight

Weight can be used to dampen vibration. The heavier your lathe and stand are, the more likely they'll be able to reduce vibration. Consider adding weight to your stand in the form of bricks or sand, as shown in the bottom photo. Bricks make less of a mess but are not as heavy as sand. Sand-filled tubes are popular, as these can be draped over legs and stand shelves to increase the weight.

Attach the stand to the floor

Many woodturners have found that an excellent way to minimize vibration is to mount their lathe stand to the shop floor, as shown in the top photo. For woods floors, simply drill pilot holes and secure the stand with lag bolts and washers. For concrete floors you'll need to drill larger holes for lag shields; then secure the stand with lag bolts and washers. This way, any stand vibration will be transferred directly into the floor.

Try adding rubber pads

If you're not interested in drilling holes in your floor, try adding rubber pads under the legs of the stand. Mail-order suppliers sell special anti-vibration padding, but we've found that a square cut from a standard foam shop floor mat works well. Just cut a piece to size and slip one pad under each leg, as shown in the middle photo.

Check the wood

If you've tried all of these techniques and your lathe still vibrates, it may be your workpiece. The wood itself may be unbalanced due to compression wood, the way the tree grew, or defect placement (knots and the like). You can check a piece for imbalance once it has been mounted on the lathe by simply giving it a spin by hand. A balanced workpiece will spin freely and continue to spin at a uniform speed until friction slows it down. An imbalanced workpiece will not spin uniformly and will tend to oscillate back and forth after you've spun it, and eventually the heavy portion of the piece will rock its way toward the lathe bed, much like a pendulum. About all you can do is trim off some of the defective or heavy wood and try again.

Shaping Lathe Tools

Lathe tools dull with use, especially if you're turning a naturally abrasive wood like teak. To sharpen a lathe tool, many turners feel they have to regrind the profile. But this isn't always the case. In many situations the tool only needs to be honed (see page 152), or if it's a scraper, burnished (see page 154). How you grind or shape a profile will depend on what sharpening gear you have on hand. The most common ways to grind profiles include freehand on a grinder (shown here), using an after-market jig with a grinder (pages 146–147), or with a wet-grinding system as described on pages 148–151. See the drawing on the opposite page for common grinding profiles and angles. Also, consider replacing the standard grinding wheel with an 80- or 100-grit aluminum oxide wheel. This type of wheel will grind a smoother surface (but will take longer to remove a lot of metal).

Tool rest setup for a gouge

To grind a gouge profile freehand, the first thing to do is to set up the tool rest. If your tool rest doesn't tilt like the Wolverine tool rest shown in the top photo, consider making a simple adjustable tilting stand and clamp it in front of the grinding wheel. The tool rest that comes standard with most grinders is virtually unusable for most lathe tool-grinding needs. To adjust the tool rest, loosen the tool rest clamp to friction-tight, and set the tool on the rest so its end makes contact with the grinding wheel, as shown in the top left photo. Then tilt it so the bevel of the gouge rests on the wheel (inset) and tighten the tool rest clamp.

Grinding a gouge freehand

Remove the tool, flip on the grinder (make sure to wear eye protection and use the grinder's guards), and present the tool tip gently to the spinning wheel. Pull back immediately and check the grind. If it isn't the correct angle, readjust the tool rest. If the grind is okay, proceed to grind the profile. For a roughing gouge, this entails simply rotating the tool against the wheel, keeping the handle perpendicular to the wheel as shown in the top right photo. For spindle and fingernail gouges, you'll have to pivot the handle from side to side as you rotate it. This takes some practice, but you can get a smooth grind as long as you keep the tool moving and use a uniform pressure.

Quench if necessary

The important thing to keep in mind as you grind a lathe tool is to do it slowly and in stages, checking the profile often. If you try to grind away too much metal at once, you can overheat the tool, causing it to loose its temper. If the tool gets too hot for you to touch, you're grinding too aggressively. If this happens, stop grinding and quench the tool tip by dipping it in a can of cool water, as shown in the bottom photo. The last thing you want to do is heat the tool up and let it gradually cool, as this will remove any heat-treating, and the metal will loose its hardness. (One of the biggest advantages to a wet-grinding system is that the tool is being constantly cooled, so this is not an issue.)

COMMON GRINDING PROFILES

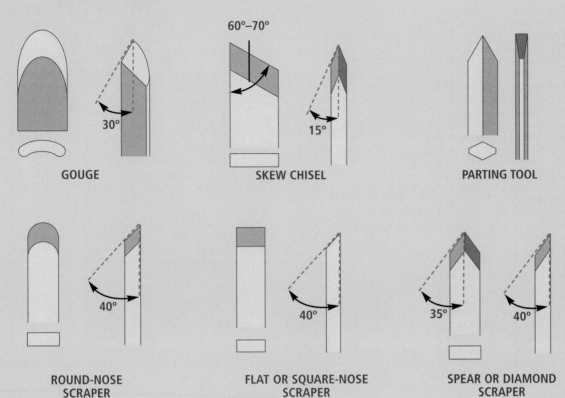

60°–70°

30°

GOUGE

15°

SKEW CHISEL

PARTING TOOL

40°

ROUND-NOSE
SCRAPER

40°

FLAT OR SQUARE-NOSE
SCRAPER

35°   40°

SPEAR OR DIAMOND
SCRAPER

MODIFIED PROFILES

SPINDLE GOUGE

30°

Front

BOWL GOUGE

60°

Front

BOWL GOUGE WITH VARIABLE SIDE GRINDS

Tool rest setup for a chisel

Setting up the tool rest to sharpen a skew chisel is similar to setting up for grinding a gouge. With the grinder off, loosen the tool rest clamp to friction-tight and press the bevel of the skew chisel against the wheel as shown in the top right photo. Then tilt the tool rest until the bevel is flat on the wheel as shown in the top left inset photo. Then tighten the tool rest clamp.

Grinding a chisel freehand

To grind a skew chisel freehand, place the tool on the tool rest so the ground profile is parallel to the wheel, as shown in the middle photo. Then turn on the grinder and gently press the tool tip into the wheel. Slide the skew chisel back and forth on the tool rest, keeping the profile parallel to the wheel. When one side is ground, flip the tool over and grind the other side with the handle angled in the opposite direction.

Setup for a scraper

Setting up a tool rest to grind a scraper is simple, as there's only one bevel to worry about. Here again, loosen the tool rest clamp and place the scraper on the rest with the tip touching the wheel as shown in the center photo. Tilt the rest as needed so the bevel is flat on the wheel (middle left inset photo) and tighten the tool rest clamp.

Grinding a scraper freehand

To grind a scraper freehand, just turn on the grinder and press the tool tip against the grinding wheel as shown in the bottom photo. For a square-nose scraper, slide the tool back and forth on the tool rest, keeping the handle perpendicular to the wheel face. With a round-nose scraper, you'll need to pivot the tool as you grind.

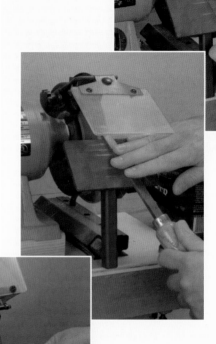

MODIFYING LATHE TOOLS

It's surprising how many woodworkers we come across who are reluctant to modify a tool to make it easier to use, more comfortable, or safer. There's a common mind-set that the tool is at its best right out of the package.

Although this is occasionally true, we frequently modify tools for the reasons stated above. Described below are modifications that we make to the lathe tools we use every day.

Modified skew. Skew chisels are so notorious for "catches" that many tool makers have started to offer a modified skew like the one shown in the top right photo with the bottom edge rounded over. This profile is illustrated on page 55 and can be ground on the grinder by first marking the desired profile and then shaping it as needed. Be aware that although the modified profile does help prevent catches, it's much more time-consuming to sharpen than a conventional skew because of the curved profile.

Corners of square-nose scrapers. If you use a square-nose scraper frequently to flatten the bottom of bowls and plates, consider knocking off just the pointed corners of the tool slightly, which are prone to digging in, as shown in the top left photo. Before you do this, realize that with that you won't be able to turn a perfectly 90-degree corner which you may need for a fine detail.

Tips of roughing gouges. The very tips of roughing gouges are also prone to digging in and catching, and so we usually grind or soften just the tips as shown in the bottom left photo. Just removing 1/16" or so of metal can dramatically reduce catches.

Sharp edges of tools. Finally, any square-shank tool can be made more comfortable and easier to use if you "ease" the square edges slightly on the grinder (bottom right photo). Skew chisels and square-nose scrapers typically have sharp edges, which are tough on the hands and which can catch on the tool rest as they're slid over the rest to make a cut. Just a slight round-over will make your hand happy and the tool a joy to use.

Grinding Jigs

The trouble with grinding lathe tools freehand on the grinder (pages 142–144) is that it's tough to get a uniform bevel, even with a steady hand and lots of practice. That's where a grinding jig comes to the rescue, like the Wolverine jig, manufactured by Oneway (www.oneway.on.ca), shown here. This jig attaches to an auxiliary base that you make and works with a standard grinder. The jig consists of a pair of base clamps that accept a long tool bar and a tool rest. Each can be slid in or out as needed. In use, the tool is placed in the V-shaped holder at the end of the long tool bar, and it's adjusted in or out to achieve the desired grind angle, as illustrated in the drawing above right. Various attachments make it easy to grind roughing, spindle, and even fingernail gouges, as well as chisels and scrapers.

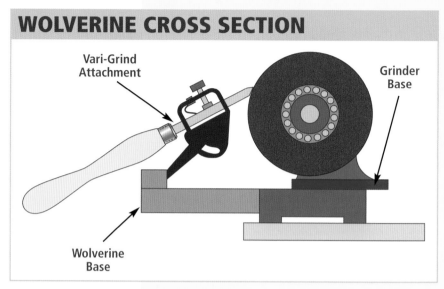

WOLVERINE CROSS SECTION

Vari-Grind Attachment

Grinder Base

Wolverine Base

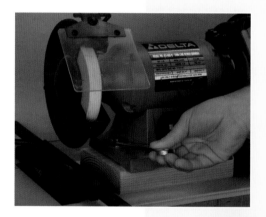

Set up the jig

To use the Wolverine jig, start by attaching your grinder and the base clamps to an auxiliary base cut from a scrap of plywood. If you use carriage bolts to attach the grinder to the plywood base, you'll need to counterbore the bottom of the base so the heads of the bolts will sit below its surface, as shown in the middle photo. Then use a wheel dresser or dressing stick to true up the face of the grinding wheel. This important step will allow you to grind a uniform profile.

Adjust the tool holder

Next, attach a tool holder if needed (like the skew chisel attachment shown in the bottom right photo) and loosen the base clamp. Now slide the long tool bar in or out so that the bevel of the tool makes full contact with the grinding wheel.

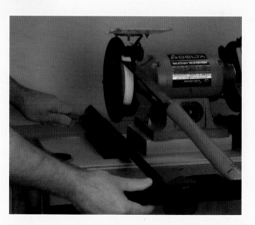

Grinding a gouge

No attachment is needed to grind a roughing or spindle gouge. Simply place the handle end in the V-shaped holder on the end of the tool bar (inset photo at right) and adjust the holder in or out so the tool's bevel makes full contact with the grinding wheel. Lift the tool tip up and turn on the grinder. Then slowly lower the tool onto the spinning wheel. Let it touch gently and then pull out the tool and inspect the grind. It should be the full width of the bevel; if it's not, readjust the tool bar and try again.

When it looks good, just rotate the tool in the holder to grind a uniform profile as shown in the top left photo. As you grind, make sure to move the tip of the gouge over the entire width of the grinding wheel to prevent grooving the wheel.

Shaping a skew chisel

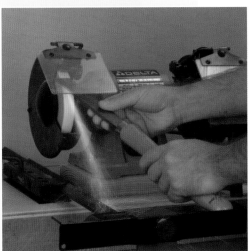

A skew chisel will require the skew-grinding attachment be added to the end of the tool bar. This long bracket has a pair of V-shaped notches at each end to hold the skew at an angle—one side for each face of the profile. After you've adjusted the tool bar for the correct bevel, turn on the grinder and place the tool in one end of the skew chisel holder. Then lower the chisel and slide the tool tip back and forth to grind the bevel as shown in the middle photo. When one side is done, move the handle to the other end of the holder and flip the chisel to grind the opposite profile.

Grinding a fingernail gouge

The complex grind of a fingernail gouge requires a more complicated holder. Wolverine's answer to this is their Vari-Grind attachment, as illustrated in the drawing on the opposite page. The gouge is clamped into the attachment with the desired length protruding. The pointed leg of the attachment fits into the V-shaped holder on the end of the tool bar. This allows you to rock the tool back and forth across the grinding wheel to grind the complex profile as shown in the bottom photo.

Water-Cooled Systems

The big risk that you run dry grinding a tool—overheating the tool so it loses its temper—is eliminated with a water-cooled grinding system like the Tormek system described here (www.tormek.com). The Tormek system consists of a large motor-driven grinding wheel that rotates slowly partially submerged in a water trough, as illustrated in the drawing below right. The end opposite the grinding wheel has a leather honing wheel that also accepts smaller curved wheels for honing the inside edge of curved tools. Mounted onto the motor case are two different sets of clamps that hold the various grinding attachments; see below. (Note: Although we only show the Tormek system sharpening lathe tools here, it's capable of sharpening a variety of tools, ranging from jointer knives to scissors.)

factory-perfect grinds with the Tormek system is their well-engineered tool holders, like the fingernail gouge and skew chisel holders shown in the top right photo.

These holders are virtually foolproof to use, guaranteeing smooth, clean pro-files. Most of their tool holders slip onto the universal support and allow you to glide the tool tip over the spinning grinding wheel.

Power-honing

Not only does the Tormek system grind tools to a very fine edge, the grinding wheel is so fine that you can take the tool directly to the power hone and hone the edge to a mirror finish as shown in the inset photo at left. The leather surfaces are first "charged" with a polishing compound (bottom photo) to speed up honing. The same attachments or tool holders you use for grinding are used to power-hone. This keeps the tool in perfect position for uniform honing.

Tool holders

One of the secrets to achieving near-

TORMEK ANATOMY

Leather Honing Wheel
Carrying Handle
Universal Support
SuperGrind Stone
Removable Water Trough
AngleMaster
Rubber Feet

Roughing gouge setup

To sharpen a roughing gouge, insert it in the appropriate tool holder and adjust the tool position so that the bevel rests on the grinding wheel, as shown in the top left photo. Once in place, lock the tool holder and universal clamps in place.

Sharpening a roughing gouge

Once the tool is set up, turn on the grinding wheel and lower the tool onto the wet surface. Rotate the tool as you glide it back and forth over the full width of the grinding wheel, as shown in the middle photo. Sliding the tool will help prevent uneven wear on the wheel. Stop and check the profile often until it is complete. Then dry off the tip and reverse the universal support so it extends out over the honing wheel. Then just slide the tool holder back onto the support and press the end into the honing wheel as shown in the top right inset photo. Rotate as you did when grinding, and also use the full width of the wheel. When you're done, remove the tool from the holder and hone the inside edge on the curved honing wheel to create a razor-sharp tool.

Skew-chisel setup

The skew-chisel tool holder is fully adjustable so that you can select not only a grinding angle, but also the skew (that is, how much the trailing edge of the chisel is angled behind the leading edge). Insert the chisel in the holder and first select the skew angle. Then slip the holder onto the universal support, and adjust for the desired grind angle as shown in the bottom photo.

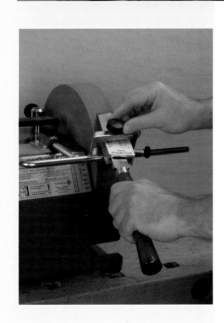

Sharpening a skew chisel

To sharpen the skew chisel, turn on the grinding system and lower the tool tip onto the wheel. Slide the tool holder back and forth slowly on the universal support to use the full width of the grinding wheel, as shown in the top right photo. After you've ground one side of the chisel, turn the chisel around and grind the other side. Then dry the tip off and flip the universal support to extend over the honing wheel. Slide the tool holder back onto the universal support, turn on the system, and power-hone the edge as shown in the top inset photo.

Scraper setup

Scrapers are one of the simplest tools to sharpen on the Tormek system, as only one angle is involved. Instead of a tool holder, there's a tool platform that attaches to the universal support that's mounted in its vertical position, as shown in the middle photo. Place your scraper on the platform and adjust it so the bevel makes full contact with the grinding wheel. You're now ready to grind.

Sharpening a scraper

To sharpen the shaper, turn on the grinding wheel and lower the tool tip onto the wheel. For a square-nose scraper, simply slide the tool back and forth on the platform, keeping the handle straight. For a round-nose scraper you'll need to pivot the tool as you slide it back and forth, as shown in the bottom photo.

The complex grind of the fingernail gouge (top inset) requires a relatively complicated tool holder. What's really nice about the Tormek gouge holder is that it's totally adjustable—you can specify not only the angle of the grind, but also the shape and length of the "wings" ground on the sides of the gouge.

Fingernail-gouge setup

To set up the bowl-gouge tool holder, start by selecting the jig setting on the side of the holder to match the shape of the profile you want to grind—that is, the shape and length of the wings. Loosen the setscrew with the Allen wrench provided, and pivot the holder to the desired setting and retighten, as shown in the upper left photo. Then extend the gouge to protrude from the jig the desired amount and lock this in place as shown in the middle inset photo. One thing we really like about this jig is once you've ground the end to a profile you like, you simply write down the jig setting and the amount of protrusion, and you can create an identical grind the next time you need to sharpen the gouge.

Sharpening a fingernail gouge

Once you've adjusted the tool holder for the desired profile, you can sharpen the gouge. Turn on the system, slide the holder onto the universal support, and place the tool tip on the wheel. Grip the adjustment wheel as shown in the lower left photo, and pivot the holder like you'd turn the page of a book, while sliding the tip gently across the grinding wheel. The holder will do all the work—it will shift the tip as necessary to grind the profile you specified. When you're done grinding, dry off the tip, flip the universal support to extend over the honing wheel, and slide the holder back on. Power-hone the outside edge as shown in the bottom inset photo. Then remove the tool from the holder and hone the inside edge on the curved honing wheel.

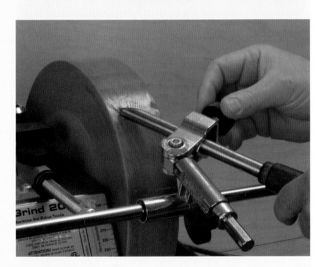

Honing Lathe Tools

Quite often all a lathe tool needs to cut cleanly is honing—not grinding. Honing can be done with oil- or waterstones or with a leather strop. The basic idea is that the tool is already ground to the correct angle but just needs the edge freshened up. You'll note that a barber uses a leather strop to achieve a keen edge on a razor—he doesn't use a grinding wheel.

Honing with a fine-grit stone

If you want to quickly fine-tune an edge, a fine-grit oil- or waterstone will do the job quickly. For oilstones, use a white or black hard Arkansas. Whether your waterstones are natural or man-made, use the finest grit you have. The idea here is not to remove a lot of metal; you just want to touch up the edge of the tool. You can hone straight-edged tools like square-nose scrapers and skew chisels by taking a few passes on a stone, as shown in the top photo—just make sure to use the proper lubricant.

Stones for outside curves

Although you can hone a curved-edge tool with a flat stone, you'll have more success with a curved stone like the one shown in the middle photo. Here again, these stones can be oil- or water-based and are available where carving tools are sold. To use a stone like this, apply the appropriate lubricant and cradle the stone in your hand as shown. Then hold the tool steady and slide the stone against the edge you're honing. If you move the tool and not the stone, it's easy to cut yourself if you slip.

Slip stones for inside edges

For an edge to be sharp, both surfaces that meet at the point must be honed. Here's where a slip stone like the one shown in the bottom photo comes in handy. Generally the curved end of these stones varies in width from end to end to fit into a variety of gouges and allows you to match the curves as well as possible. Here again, you'll want to apply a lubricant and hold the tool steady and move the stone to hone the edge.

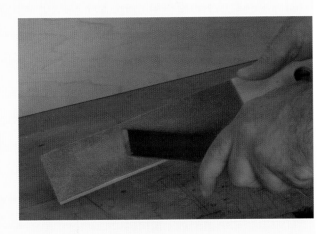

Leather strop

For even quicker touch-ups, keep a leather strop or paddle close to your lathe, like the one shown in the top photo. A paddle is a great way to quickly touch up an edge—especially a straight edge like a skew chisel. Hold the paddle still and stroke the tool back and forth on the leather surface the same number of times for each face of the tool. For faster honing action, load or charge the leather face with a polishing compound such as jeweler's rouge or Tripoli (see page 39 for more on polishing compounds).

POWER-HONING

So you've got a tool that's too dull to hone and too sharp to regrind—what do you do? Power-hone. Here's a neat way to bring up a fresh edge on almost any lathe tool. The hone itself is nothing more than a circular scrap of MDF (medium-density fiberboard) where the surface has been charged with a polishing compound. You can mount the wheel on your grinder or even your lathe.

Make and load the hone. To make a power hone, attach a rough circle of MDF to a faceplate and turn it to a diameter to fit your bench grinder. Don't sand the edge; leave it as is—it'll accept the polishing compound better this way. Remove the circle from your faceplate and drill a hole in its center to fit your grinder's arbor. Then mount it on your grinder, turn it on, and load the edge by pressing a stick of polishing compound gently to the spinning edge as shown in the upper photo at right.

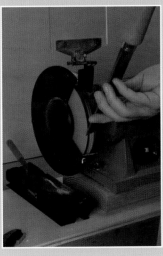

Power-honing. With the edge of the wheel loaded, you can power-hone a tool. Just make sure to present the tool tip to the wheel so that the rotation of the wheel is going away from the tool tip instead of into it, as shown in the bottom photo. If you reverse this, the tool will likely dig into the wheel (and the last thing you probably want to do is turn your grinder into a lathe). Charge the surface with polishing compound as needed—you'll notice the surface quickly turn black as you hone—this is the metal you're removing from the tool tip. If the compound builds up too much, just hold a putty knife to the edge and rotate the wheel by hand to scrape it off.

Burnishing Scrapers

Most scrapers that have been reground can be used immediately without burnishing—that's because the grinding process itself will create a burr. The only problem with this is, this burr will probably be uneven and can make it difficult to use the scraper, as the scraper will bite into the wood where the burr is large and hardly cut where it's thin. To create a uniform burr like the one illustrated in the top drawing, you'll need to burnish the tool. This can be done with a handheld burnisher or with a burnishing jig. Before you burnish a scraper, start by honing the back edge of the tool flat with an oil- or waterstone. This will remove any existing burr and create a smooth, flat surface that can rolled into a uniform burr.

Burnishing with a hand-held burnisher

Hand-held burnishers are available with round, square, or triangular shanks. If you don't have a burnisher, you can use the shank of any round tool that has been hardened (like the shank of a large-diameter drill bit or the shank of a Phillips-head screwdriver). To roll a burr on a scraper, clamp the tool in a bench vise and set the burnisher on the edge at about a 5-degree angle. Then draw the burnisher across the edge while pressing down as shown in the middle photo. Continue until you can feel a uniform burr by dragging your fingertip across the tip of the scraper.

Burnishing with a jig

If you use scrapers a lot, consider purchasing a burnishing jig like the one shown in the top photo, made by Veritas (www.leevalley.com). This jig clamps in a vise or can be mounted on a board and includes two carbide burnishing rods and a pivot pin that fit into the base. In use the scraper tip is pressed against the carbide rod and the pivot rod is used as a fulcrum to exert pressure on the rod and roll the burr, as shown in the bottom photo. This produces a keen, uniform burr.

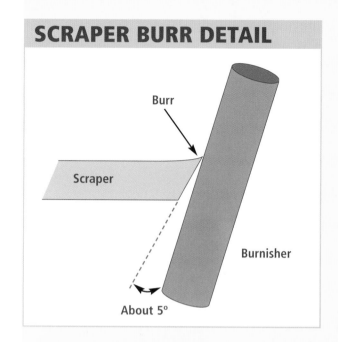

SCRAPER BURR DETAIL

Burr

Scraper

Burnisher

About 5°

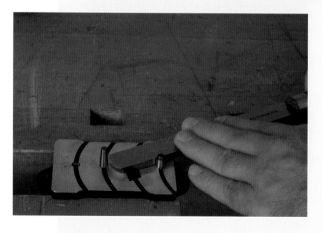

Repairing Lathe Tools

A lathe tool is more than just a sharp edge—there's the handle that accepts the tool's shank so you can control the cut. With use, handles and ferrules can come loose.

Fixing a loose handle

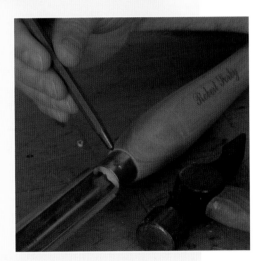

If the handle of a lathe tool becomes loose, it should be repaired immediately. The shanks of most lathe tools are press-fit into the handle and only friction keeps them in place. When a handle becomes loose, it's generally caused by shrinkage. A quick and easy remedy for this is to pull the tool out and insert a shaving into the handle hole, as shown in the top photo. Then re-insert the lathe tool and drive the shank into the handle by tapping on the tool tip with a mallet and a block of scrap wood to protect the tool edge.

Repairing a loose ferrule

A ferrule prevents a handle end from splitting when the tool is driven into the handle. Occasionally the ferrule can work loose. If it does, it likely means that the tool will work loose soon, as there isn't any pressure on the ferrule from the wood at the handle end—the wood has shrunk. Test the handle, and if it's loose, repair it as described above. If it's not, you can secure the ferrule to the handle by dimpling the ferrule with a centerpunch and a hammer, as shown in the middle photo.

Loss of temper

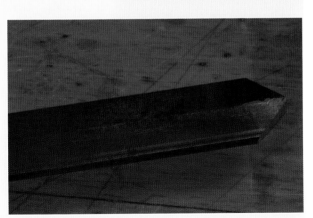

If a tool overheats from use or improper grinding, it may have lost its temper. A telltale sign of this is discolored metal at the edge, like the end of the parting tool shown in the bottom photo. And when the metal has lost its temper, it is no longer hardened. Although this makes it easier to grind, the edge will quickly dull. The only solution is to have the tool re-tempered or heat-treated. As this is an exact science, a job like this is best left to a machinist's shop or a foundry.

7 Lathe Projects

What better way to get proficient on the lathe than to start "turning" out projects? One of our favorite aspects of this versatile tool is that you can make a project from start to literally the finish on a lathe. What's more, it's the perfect tool for converting wood scraps into much-cherished gifts for family and friends.

The projects in this chapter range from simple to complex. Few projects are simpler than a turned shop mallet, but you'll still love the feel of a tool that you crafted to fit your hand. You'll find a small turned box that you can turn out in an hour, a tiered tray for holding sweets or dessert, a segmented bracelet, turned pens, a more challenging lidded box, a faux hollow-turned vessel, and a shaped-edge platter. Something for turners of all skill levels.

Just four of the many projects in this chapter are shown here: a tiered dessert tray that combines spindle with faceplate work, a challenging lidded box cut from a single blank, a segmented bracelet, and turned pens.

Shop Mallet

There are few things as enjoyable in the woodshop as using a tool that you've made—especially when you've custom-fit the tool to fit your hand, like the shop mallet shown here. The shop mallet is a perfect first project for a beginning turner, as it can be completed start to finish between centers on the lathe. We chose white oak for the mallet so it could stand up to abuse over time, although you can use almost any dense hardwood. It's also best to turn the mallet from a solid piece of wood, but if that isn't possible, glue up sufficient stock to create a 12"-long blank that's 4" square.

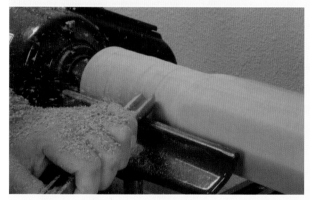

Turn a rough cylinder

Prepare the blank for mounting by drilling a centered guide hole in each end and a pair of diagonal kerfs on one end for the drive-center spurs. Since this will be a relatively large and heavy piece of wood, consider knocking off the corners to form an octagon (see page 47). Mount the blank on the lathe and adjust the tool rest. Then use a roughing gouge or spindle gouge to turn a rough cylinder, as shown in the middle photo.

SHOP MALLET PROFILE

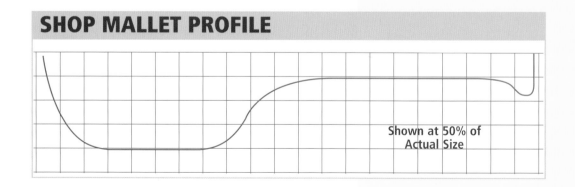

Shown at 50% of Actual Size

Lay out the shape

Once a cylinder is roughed out, you can lay out the shape on the blank. A simple way to do this is to make an enlarged copy of the pattern shown on the bottom of page 158. Then cut this out and use it as a template to mark the various transition points of the mallet, as shown in the top photo. Convert the marks into lines by turning on the lathe and touching a pencil to each mark to draw a line around the blank.

Define the shape

When you've got the lines marked on the blank, define the diameter by cutting in at each mark with a parting tool. Continue cutting until a caliper set to the desired diameter at each point just clears the spindle, as shown in the middle photo. Repeat for each transition point.

Turn the mallet

Now that you've defined the various diameters at the transition points, go ahead and turn the mallet shape, using a spindle gouge as shown in the bottom photo. Clean up any rough surfaces with a sharp skew chisel or scraper, and then sand the surface smooth. Apply a finish (if desired), remove the mallet, and cut off the waste at each end of the mallet.

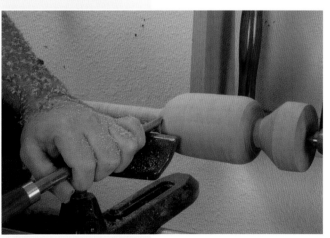

Small Bowl

Small bowls like the ones shown in the top photo are a fun and relaxing project. This is a great project for those little blocks of wood you just can't get yourself to throw away. Their diminutive size makes them easy to turn, as typical inside depth is only around 2". And they're very useful for holding loose change and small items like jewelry. You can use one of the profiles shown on the opposite page or just let a bowl take shape on the lathe. Either way, once you've turned one of these, you'll likely find yourself turning multiples for family and friends.

Attach blank to screw chuck

To make a small bowl, start by cutting a blank round and drill a centered hole for a screw chuck. Then screw the blank onto the screw chuck as shown in the middle photo. If you don't have a screw chuck, you can also mount the blank to your faceplate. With a piece this small, you can often get by with just double-sided tape in lieu of screws.

Turn exterior

With the blank on the lathe, the next step is to turn the exterior. Start by creating a rough cylinder, and then remove waste as needed to define the shape. A spindle gouge works best for this, as shown in the bottom photo. If you're working from a template or pattern, stop frequently to check your progress. After you've defined the shape, clean up any rough surfaces with a sharp scraper or skew chisel; then sand the exterior smooth.

Cut recess for scroll chuck

All that's left to do with the blank in this position is to true up the bottom and cut a recess for your scroll chuck. A square-nose scraper will make quick work of truing the bottom. Then cut the recess to fit your scroll chuck. Start by marking the recess location on the bottom. Then define the perimeter and recess depth with a parting tool. Remove the waste in the recess and flatten the bottom with a square-nose scraper. Finally, define the angled perimeter wall to match the angle of your scroll chuck jaws, using a dovetail scraper or a skew chisel, as shown in the top photo. When complete, sand the bottom smooth.

Mount on scroll chuck

Turn off the lathe and remove the blank and faceplate or screw chuck from the headstock spindle. Then remove the blank from the screw chuck or faceplate. Mount your scroll chuck onto the lathe and then mount the blank onto the scroll chuck as shown in the middle photo. Tighten the jaws to hold the blank firmly, and rotate the chuck by hand to make sure it's mounted square in the chuck.

SMALL BOWL PROFILES

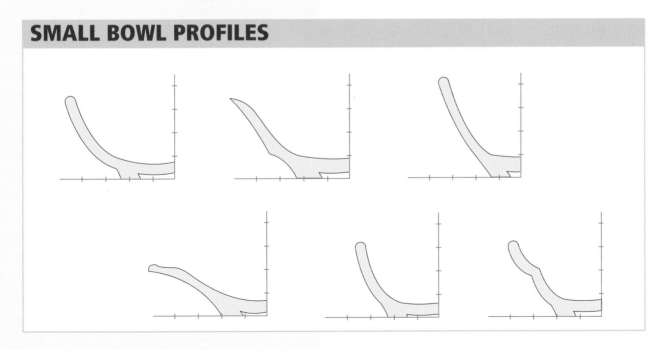

Turn the interior

All that's left is to turn and smooth the interior. We generally use a spindle gouge to remove the bulk of the waste, as shown in the top photo. Even with a blank this small, it's still a good idea to leave a cone in the center of the blank to help keep it balanced and minimize vibration. When the majority of the waste has been removed, go ahead and remove the center cone.

Smooth the walls

How smooth the interior is at this point will depend on how sharp your gouge is, your technique, and the type of wood you're using. Some squirrelly woods tend to tear even when a sharp gouge is used. You may find that light cuts with a freshly burnished scraper will do a better job of cleaning up the walls, as shown in the middle photo. Light cuts with little applied pressure is what you're after here.

Flatten the bottom (if desired)

If your bowl design calls for a flat bottom, consider switching to a square-nose scraper to get a super-flat bottom, as shown in the bottom photo. Take light cuts and stop when you approach the curved transition to the walls so you don't accidentally cut into the curve. When the interior is complete, sand if necessary. Then apply the finish of your choice before removing the bowl from the scroll chuck.

Tiered Tray

A tiered tray like the one shown in the top photo combines basic spindle work with simple faceplate work to create a tray that's both elegant and useful.

What's really nice is that you can get the entire project out of a single 6"-wide piece of 3/4"-thick stock that's only 10" long. The tiered tray consists of a top and bottom tray connected by a bottom spindle and topped with a handle, as illustrated in the drawing below. The parts are held solidly together via round tenons and mortises. The tenon on the handle passes through the top tray and into a mortise drilled into the top of the bottom spindle. For as delicate as this looks, it's surprisingly sturdy.

TIERED TRAY PROFILES

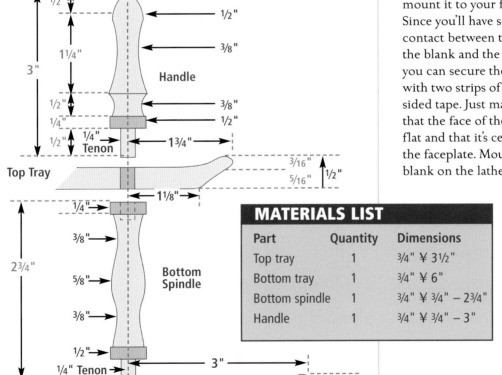

MATERIALS LIST

Part	Quantity	Dimensions
Top tray	1	3/4" ¥ 3½"
Bottom tray	1	3/4" ¥ 6"
Bottom spindle	1	3/4" ¥ 3/4" – 2¾"
Handle	1	3/4" ¥ 3/4" – 3"

Turn the bottom tray

To make the tiered tray, start with the faceplate work. Cut a rough circular blank to size for the bottom tray and mount it to your faceplate. Since you'll have so much contact between the face of the blank and the faceplate, you can secure the blank with two strips of double-sided tape. Just make sure that the face of the blank is flat and that it's centered on the faceplate. Mount the blank on the lathe, and true up and shape the rim. Reposition the tool rest and turn the inside of the tray as shown in the middle photo. Create a flat bottom with a square-nose scraper.

Turn the top tray

Remove the bottom tray from your faceplate and attach a circular blank for the top tray. True up and shape the rim. Then turn the inside as shown in the top photo. You can follow the profile shown on page 163 or create your own. When the top tray is shaped, sand it smooth and remove it from the faceplate and remove the faceplate from the lathe.

Turn the bottom spindle

With the trays complete, you can turn your attention to the spindle work. Start by mounting a blank for the bottom spindle between centers of the lathe. Turn the blank round and mark the transition points on the spindle with a pencil. Define the diameters at the transition points with a parting tool and calipers. Then turn the profile as shown in the middle photo. Take care in sizing the tenons (see the wrench tip on page 62) and when done, sand the profile smooth. Remove the workpiece and cut the waste ends off with a handsaw.

Turn the handle

Next, mount a blank for the handle between centers. Turn it round, lay out and define the profile, and then turn the shape as shown in the bottom photo. A small-spindle gouge (1/4" or so) works best for defining the small, fine details. Remove the blank and cut off the waste ends.

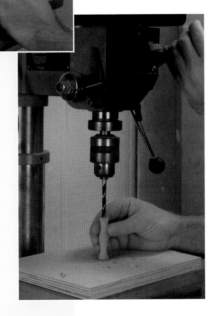

Drill holes in the trays

Now that all the parts have been turned, you can begin assembly. Start by laying out centered holes in the bottoms of both trays. The drill a 1/4"-diameter hole through the top tray and a stopped 1/4"-diameter hole in the bottom tray as shown in the top photo.

Drill a mortise in the bottom spindle

Next, drill a hole in the top of the bottom spindle to accept the tenon on the bottom of the handle. Make sure to accurately mark the hole location, and then centerpunch this to keep the drill bit from wandering. The most accurate way to hold the spindle straight is to drill a hole in a scrap of wood to match the diameter of the tenon on the end of the bottom spindle. Then insert the tenon in the scrap and drill the hole, using one hand to steady the spindle, as shown in the middle photo.

Assemble the tray

To assemble the tray, start by applying glue to the tenon on the bottom spindle. Then insert this in the mortise in the bottom tray. Next, apply glue to the tenon on the end of the handle. Press the tenon through the mortise in the top tray and into the mortise on top of the bottom spindle, as shown in the bottom photo. Allow the glue to dry overnight before using the tray.

Segmented Bracelet

Although you could turn a bracelet out of a single piece of wood, you'd quickly learn the folly of this. For starters, bracelets tend to be thin and delicate, and a solid-wood version would have two areas that consisted mainly of end grain. These areas would be so weak that it'd be easy to snap the bracelet in half. Even the simple act of putting it on could cause it to break as it's being slid over the hand and onto the wrist. Second, it wouldn't stay round very long, since the exposed end grain would shrink and long grain would stay relatively stable, resulting in an oval.

The solution to both of these problems is to make a bracelet by first gluing up segments to form a stronger, more stable blank. If you use the cutting and gluing sequence described here, you'll end up with a strong bracelet that's easy to turn.

Cut the segments to length

To create a segmented blank for a bracelet, start with a long strip of wood that's 3/4" ¥ 3/4". Then make a simple cutting jig to attach to the miter gauge of your table saw. This jig is nothing more than a strip of wood with a 45-degree stop block on one end, as shown in the middle photo. Attach the jig to your miter gauge angled to 45 degrees so it will cut a segment that's roughly 13/4" long from long point to long point.

As you make your first cut, grip and push the segment along with the eraser end of a pencil, as shown in the middle photo. Note the use of a spring clamp to hold the strip in place for the cut. Move the cut segment and jig completely past the saw blade. Remove the cut segment and rotate the strip as illustrated in the drawing below to cut the next segment. You'll need eight segments for each bracelet.

SEGMENT-CUTTING SEQUENCE

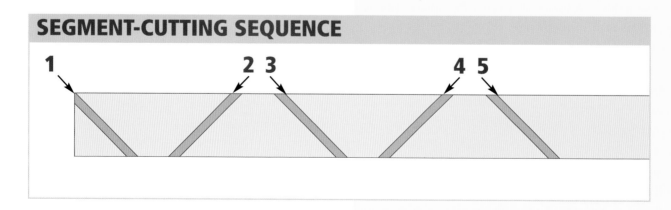

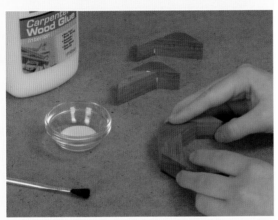

Glue up pairs of segments

Once the segments are cut, you can begin gluing up the bracelet. Since these pieces are small and angled, the best way to glue them up is by using your hands as clamps. Apply a generous amount of glue to the end grain of one segment and position this against another segment, as illustrated in the drawing below. Hold the pieces still for 2 minutes while applying moderate pressure with your hands. After 2 minutes, gently set the glued-up pair aside and allow it to dry completely. Repeat for the remaining segments until you have four glued-up pairs.

Glue pairs into halves

When the glue has dried in the pairs, you can glue pairs up to create two halves. Use the same gluing and pressing technique to glue up two sets of pairs into two halves as shown in the middle photo. Set these aside to dry.

Glue the halves together

Before you glue the halves together, check to make sure they mate nicely together. If there's any gap, sand one or both ends to eliminate the gap. A belt/disk sander and a miter gauge work best for this, but you can also do it by hand with a sanding block or a fine mill file. When the fit is perfect, glue the two halves together using the same technique described above and shown in the bottom photo. Allow the glue to dry completely before proceeding.

SEGMENT PROFILLE

Attach the blank to a scrap block

When the bracelet blank is completely dry, the next step is to attach it to a faceplate so that you can turn the interior walls. Since you'll need to cut through the entire width of the blank, you'll need to first mount the blank to a scrap block as shown in the top photo. This way you can cut right into the scrap block as needed. To make separating the blank from the scrap block easy, sandwich a layer of kraft paper between the blank and the block when you glue it on, as shown in the top photo.

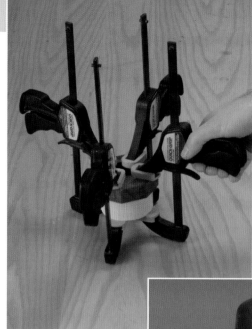

Attach the blank to your faceplate

After the glue has dried, you can attach the scrap block/blank to your faceplate. Take your time here to center the blank on the faceplate. If you mount it off-center, you'll end up with a bracelet that has uneven segments and you may not be able to get the desired-diameter bracelet out of the blank. When it's centered, drive screws through the faceplate and into the scrap block as shown in the middle photo.

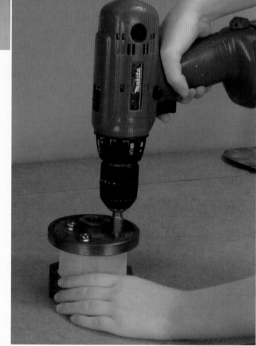

Turn the interior walls

Now you can mount the blank on your lathe and turn the interior walls. The simplest way to define the interior walls is to cut into the face of the blank with a parting tool as shown in the bottom photo. Make sure that you cut through the full width of the blank and into the scrap block. If this cut is rough, you can usually clean it up by taking a light cut with a skew chisel or square-nose scraper by simply pressing the tool tip straight into the face as you did with the parting tool.

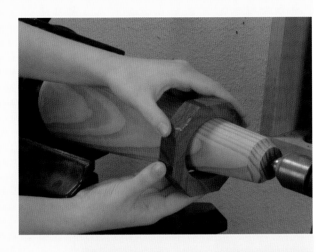

Transfer the blank to a mandrel chuck

As soon as the interior walls are turned round, remove the faceplate and separate the blank from the scrap block with a sharp chisel. Then mount a tapered mandrel chuck onto the lathe (see pages 104–105 for step-by-step directions on how to make one of these). Slip the bracelet over the narrow end of the chuck as shown in the top photo, and slide it down until it binds. Make sure it's squarely on the chuck by rotating the mandrel by hand. If you see that it wobbles, it's not on straight and needs to be repositioned. Note: Make sure the blank is on the chuck so that the glue joints of the blank rotate away from a lathe tool instead of into it. A blank where the glue joints rotate into the tool tip is prone to splitting at the joint.

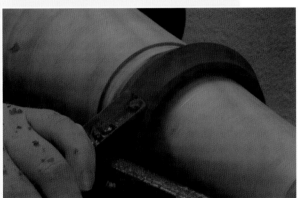

Turn the exterior profile

All that's left is to turn the exterior profile. You can use one of the profiles illustrated in the drawing below or make up your own. A small-spindle gouge ($^1/4$" or $^3/8$") works well for most shaping. Once you've completed the profile, sand if necessary and apply the finish of your choice before slipping the bracelet off the mandrel.

COMMON BRACELET PROFILES

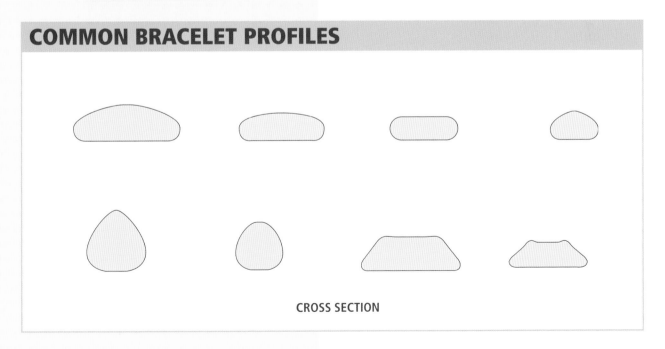

CROSS SECTION

Turned Pens

Turned pens have become such a popular lathe project that some manufacturers make a lathe specifically for turning pens (page 12). It's quite understandable why they're so popular: They're both attractive (top photo) and easy to make. Especially since savvy accessory makers have started offering pen kits, pen-making mandrels, and bushings to make it easy to turn a variety of pens. Most mail-order woodworking catalogs sell supplies, along with numerous species of blanks and even pre-drilled blanks. A pen kit is the easiest way to get into pen making and contains all the parts you need to make a pen; see the drawings and materials list on the opposite page. Although many different pen styles can be turned on a single mandrel, you'll need to purchase different sets of bushings for each style.

Cut the blanks to length

You can either purchase pen blanks or make your own. If you make your own, you'll want a blank that's roughly 5/8" square and 6" long. The first step to making a pen is to cut this blank into a long and short blank to correspond to the lengths of the short and long tubes that come with the kit. These tubes are glued into the blanks and accept the pen parts. Most kit makers suggest you cut the blanks a bit long and then sand the ends until they're flush with the tubes. Since these are small pieces, it's best to clamp them in place when you cut them as shown in the bottom left photo.

Drill tube holes

The next step is to drill holes through the length of each blank with the drill bit specified by the manufacturer. Many kits specify a 7mm drill bit. The easiest way to get a straight hole through a vertically held blank is to clamp it in between the jaws of a woodscrew, as shown in the upper right photo. Clamp the blank friction-tight, and then use a small square to position it so that it's perfectly plumb in the clamp jaws before tightening (bottom right photo). Then mark the center of the blank and drill a hole though its length.

PEN ANATOMY

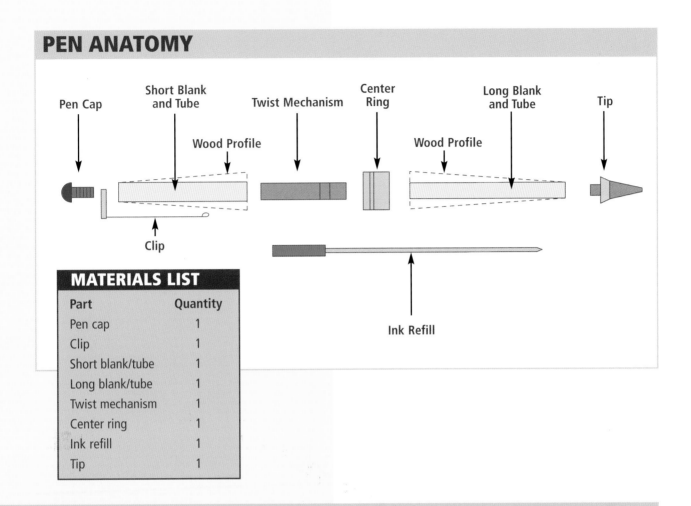

Pen Cap

Short Blank and Tube

Wood Profile

Clip

Twist Mechanism

Center Ring

Long Blank and Tube

Wood Profile

Tip

Ink Refill

MATERIALS LIST

Part	Quantity
Pen cap	1
Clip	1
Short blank/tube	1
Long blank/tube	1
Twist mechanism	1
Center ring	1
Ink refill	1
Tip	1

PEN KITS

Pen kits supply all the hardware you need to assemble a pen, as shown at right. All you need to supply is the wood for the two blanks and the mandrel system and bushings to match the pen kit. The brass tubes are glued into holes you drill in the wood blanks with a special brad-point bit you'll also need, which is sized to accept the tubes. The tubes/blanks are then placed on the mandrel along with the bushings, and this is mounted on the lathe for turning. After turning the profiles, you'll remove the blanks from the mandrel and press the pen parts into place on the blanks as you assemble the pen.

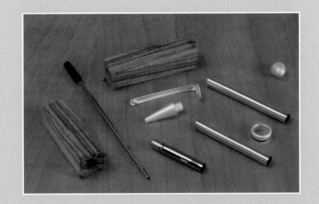

Prepare the tubes

With the holes drilled, you can glue a corresponding brass tube into each blank. Before you do this, it's a good idea to rough up the exterior of each tube with a piece of emery cloth or with silicon-carbide sandpaper, as shown in the top photo. Roughing up the exterior like this gives the glue something to grab onto, versus having a smooth and shiny exterior. Don't go overboard here—all it takes is a couple of strokes. Just do enough so the surface is no longer glossy.

Glue the tubes in the blanks

Now you can glue the tubes in. Cyanoacrylate or "instant" glue is what you want to use here. We found the best way to get a good glue-up is to temporarily clamp a drilled blank to the edge of the workbench so its end extends off the bench a bit, as shown in the middle photo. Then place just the very end of the tube in the hole and drip one or two drops of instant glue onto the tube. Quickly slide the tube into the hole, rotating the tube as you do this to spread the glue evenly around the tube as it slides in. Press it in until it's flush or slightly below the end. Repeat this for the other blank and tube.

Mount the blanks on the mandrel

Since this glue dries instantly, you can immediately mount the blanks onto the mandrel. If the ends of the blanks aren't perfectly flush with the tubes, sand the ends until they are (a belt/disk sander with a miter gauge to hold the blank is the most reliable way to get a square end). Then follow the kit's instructions as to what bushings go where on the mandrel, with respect to the short and long blanks. In most cases, it's bushing—blank—bushing—blank—bushing. Once they're in place, mount the mandrel on your lathe and tighten the nut on the end of the mandrel to snug up the blanks and bushings, as shown in the bottom photo.

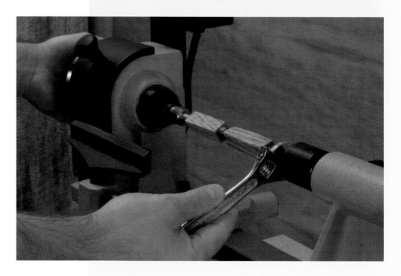

Turn the blanks to a rough cylinder

Now you're ready to turn. Start by positioning your tool rest as close to the blanks as possible, and then turn on the lathe. Use a roughing or spindle gouge to quickly turn both blanks into rough cylinders, as shown in the top photo. If you notice that one or both of the blanks catch and spin on the mandrel instead of spinning with the mandrel, stop the lathe and tighten the nut on the ends of the mandrel another turn or two.

Turn the tenon

For the pen shown here, a tenon needs to be turned on one end of the short blank to accept a loose bushing that fits over the center bushing. Use a parting tool, as shown, to turn the tenon until the bushing can be press-fit onto the tenon. Remove wood very slowly and check the fit often, as it's very easy to remove too much wood.

Turn the short and long profiles

With the loose bushing in place (if applicable), turn the profiles on the short blank (bottom left photo) and long blank (bottom inset photo). The bushings make this easy, as all you have to do is remove wood from each end until it's flush with the bushing. Then for the short blank, turn the recommended profile. For the long blank, turn a long uniform taper from the wide end to the narrow end.

Sand the blanks

Depending on the wood you're using and the sharpness of your tools, you may or may not need to sand the blanks smooth. If you need to, fold a small piece of 150-grit sandpaper in two and sand each profile smooth, taking care to first remove the tool rest. As most turners want a very smooth surface

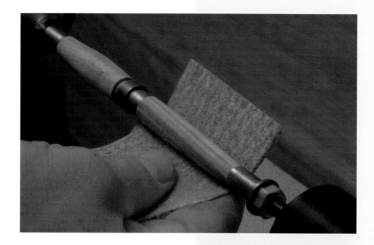

on their pens, you'll need to work your way up slowly, with increasingly finer grits. We've found that sanding up to 600 grit produces a very satisfactory surface. Be sure to blow off or vacuum the blanks between grits to prevent bits of loose grit from scratching the surface.

Apply a finish

When you're satisfied with the surface smoothness, you can apply a finish. For the pens here we used a liquid finish that uses friction to flow the finish onto the surface, producing a high gloss, as shown in the middle photo. For more on friction finishes, see page 75. Take care when applying this to wipe off immediately any that gets onto the bushings. Besides creating a high gloss, this finish has the added benefit of drying almost instantly as you buff it.

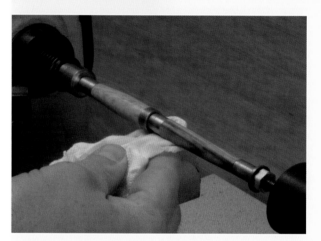

Remove the blanks from the mandrel

If you used a quick-drying finish like the friction finish described above, you can immediately remove the turned blanks from the mandrel. Just loosen the nut on the end of the mandrel and slide all of the parts off, as shown in the bottom photo. If you used a conventional finish that needs some dry time, set the mandrel aside or leave it in place on the lathe as the parts dry.

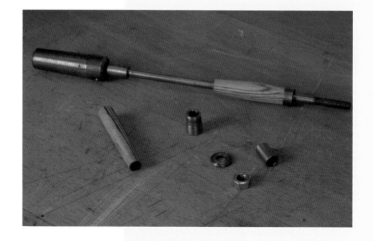

Attach the pen parts to the top

Now you can begin assembling the pen. Consult the pen kit maker's instructions for the specific procedure for your pen kit. For the one shown here, we started by pressing the clip and cap onto the end of the pen. A reliable way to do this is to put the blank and pen parts between the jaws of your bench vise and then slowly close the jaws to press the parts into the end of the brass tube, as shown in the top photo.

Attach the pen parts to the bottom

Next, press the tip onto the narrow end of the long blank as you did for the top of the pen (middle photo). If your pen has a center ring like the one shown here, you'll need to glue the center ring onto the end of one of the blanks; consult your kit directions for recommended placement.

Assemble the pen

To complete the pen assembly, you'll press the twist mechanism into the top or short blank so that it protrudes the recommended amount. Then slide in the ink refill and connect the top and bottom halves as shown in the bottom photo. Twist the top to make sure the tip of the ink refill protrudes the recommended amount. If it doesn't, you'll need to readjust the position of the twist mechanism; consult the kit maker's instructions on the best way to do this.

Lidded Box

When you're ready for a challenging but rewarding turning project, consider turning a lidded box like the one shown in the top photo. Lidded boxes can be made almost any size, but smaller ones like the version shown here are popular because they don't require a lot of wood and are easier to turn. Smaller lidded boxes are also more popular since both the lid and box are turned from the same piece—larger blanks of solid wood like this are not as easy to come by as smaller blanks, and smaller blanks cost a lot less. The box shown here is turned from a single 4" square block that's roughly 5" long. Please note that the profile shown on the opposite page is just a suggestion, and you can turn any shape that pleases you. What makes this project especially challenging is that the fit of the lid on the box must be perfect as the top profile is shaped while the lid is held in place on the bottom by friction only.

the blank and then fitting this tenon inside the jaws of the chuck. This way when we tightened the jaws, they constricted to securely grip the tenon, as shown in the bottom left photo. Note that we covered the exposed ends of the jaws with a rubber band to serve as a cushion in case hands or tools accidentally make contact with the unforgiving steel.

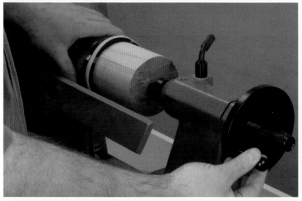

Mount the blank in a chuck

To make a lidded box, start by preparing the blank. How you do this will depend on what chuck you'll be using to hold the workpiece. Because one end of the blank is unsupported for the bulk of the turning, you'll want a really secure method to hold the blank. We chose to mount it in our scroll chuck, by first turning a tenon on the end of

Slide the tailstock over for support

As we've recommended numerous times, anytime you can use the tailstock for added support, do so. Slide the tailstock over and adjust the center for a press-fit against the exposed end of the blank, as shown in the middle photo.

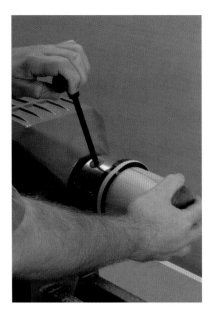

BOX PROFILE

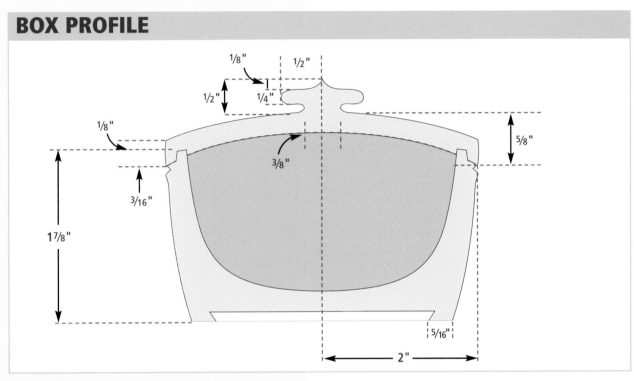

1/8 "
1/2 "
1/2 "
1/4 "
1/8 "
3/8 "
5/8 "
3/16 "
1⁷/8 "
5/16 "
2 "

SHAPING THE BOX: STEPS 1–5

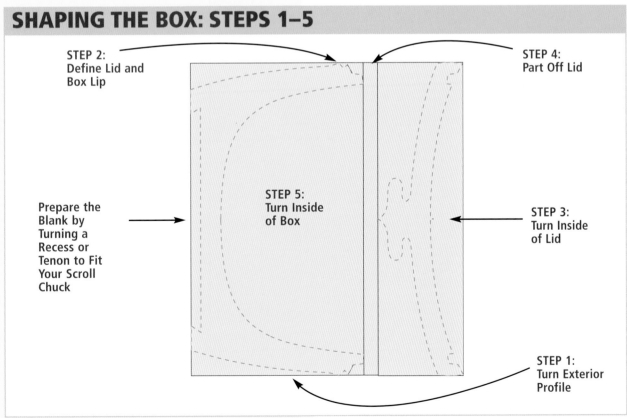

STEP 2:
Define Lid and
Box Lip

STEP 4:
Part Off Lid

Prepare the
Blank by
Turning a
Recess or
Tenon to Fit
Your Scroll
Chuck

STEP 5:
Turn Inside
of Box

STEP 3:
Turn Inside
of Lid

STEP 1:
Turn Exterior
Profile

Turn the box profile

Now you can turn the exterior profile of the box; see the profile and the drawing illustrating the steps for making your initial cuts on page 177. Begin by marking the top of the box, and then shape the profile with a spindle or fingernail gouge as shown in the top photo. Stop frequently to check the profile against the pattern or template that you're using (if applicable). When you're done shaping, smooth the surface with a skew chisel or a freshly burnished scraper and sand if necessary.

Define the lid and box lip

Once the exterior of the box is complete, use a parting tool to define the end of the lid and also the lip of the box, as shown in the middle photo. Leave the lip a bit on the fat side, as you'll tweak this for a perfect fit once the lid interior has been shaped and the lid has been parted off.

Turn the inside of the lid

At this point you'll need to slide the tailstock away from the blank so you can turn the inside profile of the lid. Adjust the tool rest to sit close to the end of the blank, and use a spindle gouge or a round-nose scraper to hollow out the inside of the lid, as shown in the bottom photo. Remember that since this end of the blank is unsupported, it's important to use sharp tools and take light cuts. When you've hollowed out the inside, define the lid lip with a parting tool.

Part off the lid

Now for some fun. It's time to part the lid off the blank. Make a series of cuts to the waste side of the box top with a parting tool, as shown in the top photo. To prevent the parting tool from overheating, widen the kerf slightly as you cut to keep it from binding. As you get near the center of the blank, hold the parting tool with one hand and use your other hand to gently cradle the spinning lid—just make sure to keep your fingers away from the tool rest to prevent a nasty pinch (or worse). When you cut completely through, the lid will simply fall off into your hand. Set the lid aside; you'll finish it after you've scooped out the interior of the box.

Hollow the inside of the box

Reposition your tool rest so it's facing the end of the blank, and use a spindle gouge or round-nose scraper to hollow out the inside of the box. A heavy-duty round-nose scraper like the one shown in the middle photo is ideal for this work. Its thick shank is very stable when extended out past the tool rest and so is easy to control, as it won't vibrate like a thinner scraper can. When the box is hollowed, sand the interior if necessary.

SHAPING THE BOX: STEPS 6–8

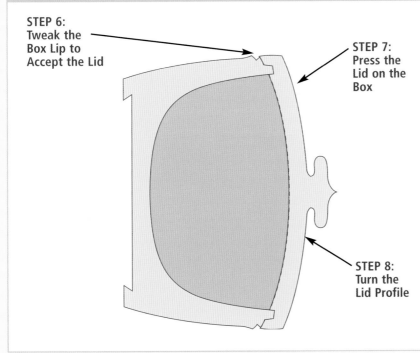

STEP 6:
Tweak the
Box Lip to
Accept the Lid

STEP 7:
Press the
Lid on the
Box

STEP 8:
Turn the
Lid Profile

Tweak the box lip

The box portion of the project is basically done at this point, and now it's time to finish the lid; see the drawing on page 179 for the recommended sequence of cuts. To begin work on the lid, first check to see if it fits on the box. Odds are it won't since you intentionally left the box lid lip a bit fat. Use a parting tool or flat-nose scraper to tweak the lip so the lid can just barely be pressed onto it, as shown in the top photo. Stop frequently and check this. If you remove too much wood, you'll have to make either a new box or a new lid, so take your time here. You want a tight friction fit, as this is all that holds the lid on the box for its final shaping.

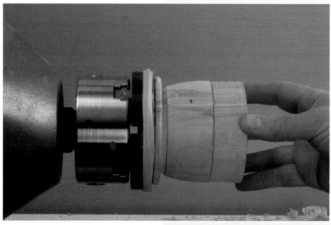

Replace lid on box

Once you've tweaked the box lid lip as needed, press the lid firmly onto the box so that it bottoms out on the box and there's no gap between the two pieces, as shown in the middle photo. Before you turn the lid profile, you can use a skew chisel, parting tool, or diamond-point scraper to cut a slight relief where the two parts meet. This relief will hide any imperfections at the joint; see the box profile on page 177.

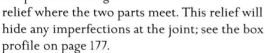

Turn the lid profile

All that's left is to turn the profile of the lid top. If you've got a lot of material to remove, slide the tailstock over to help keep the lid pressed firmly on the box as shown in the bottom photo. Turn as much of the profile as possible this way and then remove the tailstock. Complete the profile by taking a series of very light cuts, and apply the finish of your choice.

Faux Hollow-Turned Vessel

Many woodturners consider a hollow-turned vessel as the ultimate turning project. There are some pro turners who turn only these. They craft delicate vases with tiny necks—yet the inside has been hollowed. How to do they do this? With crooked-neck scrapers, various jigs, a lot of patience, hours of practice, and many, many broken vessels. If you'd like to turn one of these but don't want to invest the money for special tools and the time needed to master the skills required, consider shaping a faux hollow-turned vessel like the one shown in the top photo. No special tools are required, yet the piece appears to have been turned from a solid piece of wood and decorated with a band of inlay. In reality, two separate halves are turned, hollowed, and then joined together with a half-lap joint, as illustrated by the drawings on page 182. Then this joint is covered with an inlay.

Turn the bottom profile

Start work on your faux hollow-turned vessel by mounting a circular blank to your faceplate. Mount this on the lathe. Then true the rim and shape the bottom profile as shown in the middle left photo. Next, slide the tool rest over and true up the bottom. Cut a recess to fit your scroll chuck as shown in the inset photo above right.

Mount the blank on a scroll chuck

Turn off the lathe and remove the blank from the headstock spindle. Unscrew the faceplate from the blank and mount your scroll chuck on the lathe. Then slip the recess in the bottom of the blank over the jaws of the scroll chuck so the piece bottoms out on the jaws, and tighten the jaws to hold the blank as shown in the bottom photo.

Hollow out the bottom

Now you can position the tool rest in front of the face of the blank and hollow out the inside, using a spindle gouge as shown in the top photo or a round-nose scraper. You'll be removing a lot of wood here, so stop frequently to check the profile and clear away shavings. Whichever tool you use, leave a cone in the center of the blank to help stabilize it and reduce vibration. When you've finished shaping the walls, go back and remove the cone.

FAUX-VESSEL PROFILE

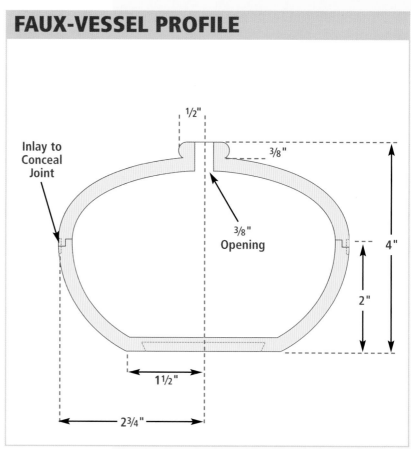

Inlay to Conceal Joint

1/2"

3/8"

3/8" Opening

4"

2"

1½"

2¾"

FAUX-VESSEL JOINT

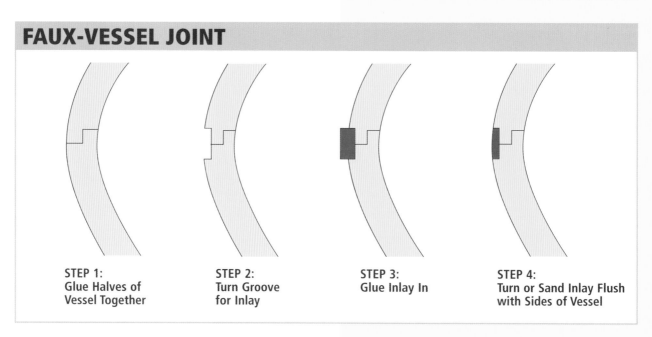

STEP 1:
Glue Halves of Vessel Together

STEP 2:
Turn Groove for Inlay

STEP 3:
Glue Inlay In

STEP 4:
Turn or Sand Inlay Flush with Sides of Vessel

Turn the lip for the half-lap joint

All that's left on the bottom portion of the vessel is to shape the lip, which will be one-half of the half-lap joint, as illustrated on page 182. Cut the lip with a parting tool, skew chisel, or square-nose scraper as shown in the top photo. Turn off the lathe, and remove the blank and then the scroll chuck.

Hollow out the inside of the top

Begin work on the top half of the vessel by attaching a circular blank to your faceplate. Mount the faceplate on the lathe, and position the tool rest in front of the face of the blank. Then hollow out the inside profile of the top piece using a spindle gouge or a round-nose scraper as shown in the middle photo. Stop frequently to check what you've turned versus the pattern or template you're following (if applicable).

Cut the other half of the half-lap joint

Once the inside of the top has been hollowed out, you can cut the other half of the half-lap joint. Cut this with a parting tool or a square-nose scraper as shown in the bottom photo. Make sure to stop frequently and check to see whether the bottom will fit onto the top. Since this needs to be a tight joint, it's imperative that you stop after you've taken just a whisper of a shaving when you get the joint close to fitting. When the fit is friction-tight, you've cut it perfectly.

Glue the halves together

At this point you're ready to join the two halves together. To do this, spread a generous coat of glue onto both halves of the half-lap joint and press the two pieces together. You can use the lathe as a clamp by sliding the tailstock over and pressing a disk of scrap wood into the assembly, as shown in the top photo. Lock the tailstock down firmly, and then adjust the tailstock (minus the center) over to press the two halves together. Let this sit overnight.

Remount on scroll chuck

After the glue has dried, slide the tailstock away from the blank and remove it from the lathe. Unscrew the faceplate and mount your scroll chuck on the lathe. Then fit the recess in the bottom over the jaws of the scroll chuck and tighten the jaws as shown in the middle right photo.

Turn the top profile

Now you can turn the profile on the top of the vessel. Reposition the tailstock to better support the blank (middle left photo), and shape the top profile with a spindle gouge or scraper as shown in the bottom photo. Stop and check your profile often. The last thing you want to do is cut through the thin exterior wall. When the profile is complete, you can sand the exterior if needed.

Cut the groove for the inlay

All that's left is to add the inlay and touch up the opening at the top of the vessel. Lay out a groove centered on the half-lap joint to match the width of your inlay, and then cut the groove with a parting tool as shown in the top photo. Start by cutting the groove just a bit narrower than the inlay, and slowly widen it until the inlay just fits (inset photo below). As for the groove depth, cut it a bit less than the thickness of your inlay. This way you can trim it flush after the glue has dried. In order to wrap around the vessel, you'll want the inlay to be about $1/8$" to $3/16$"thick. You can purchase inlay or make your own.

Add the inlay

With the groove cut, you can cut your inlay to length to fit in the groove. This will take some patience, as it's best to cut the inlay long and slowly trim it to a perfect fit. Instead of butting the ends of the inlay strip together, miter the ends to create a scarf joint so the joint will be almost invisible. If you do this, you'll want to glue the inlay in the groove so that top long miter of the joint faces opposite the direction of the workpiece rotation. This will ensure that you won't catch the edge with a turning tool when you trim the inlay flush. The best tool to hold the inlay in place as it dries is a band clamp like that shown in the middle photo.

Finish the profile

Allow the glue to dry overnight before removing the clamp. First trim the inlay flush, then finish the neck of the vessel as shown in the bottom photo. You can leave the tailstock in place until the very end. Then slide it away and either drill a hole in the neck or cut a hole with a small spindle gouge or parting tool. Sand the piece completely, and apply the finish of your choice.

Shaped-Edge Platter

Platters have always been a favorite of ours, as they're easy to turn and only require a single square of wood. To add a touch of distinction to a platter, try turning a wide rim and then removing some of this to create a shaped-edge platter like the one shown in the top photo and illustrated in the drawing on the opposite page. You can turn the platter from a solid piece of stock, or create an interesting pattern by gluing up a blank as we did here. We sandwiched maple veneer between strips of walnut for visual interest (for more on glued-up blanks, see page 96).

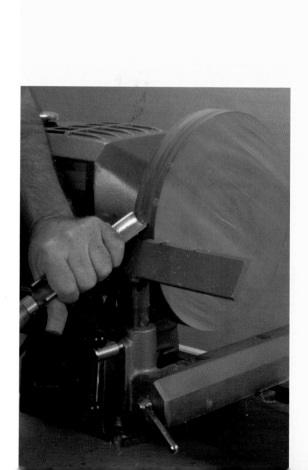

Attach the blank to a faceplate
To make a shaped-edge platter, start by cutting the blank to a rough circle shape. Then attach a faceplate to what will become the face or inside of the platter, as shown in the middle photo. Make sure to use as many screws as there are holes in the faceplate.

True the rim
Next, mount the faceplate and blank on the lathe. Position the tool rest in front of the rim and use a roughing gouge or spindle gouge to true up the rim as shown in the bottom photo.

Shape the rim

Once the rim has been trued, go ahead and lay out the desired profile on the blank with a pencil. Then use a spindle gouge or fingernail gouge to remove the bulk of the waste, taking care to stop frequently and check your profile against the pattern or template you're using (if applicable). Finish off the rim profile by taking light cuts with a freshly burnished scraper as shown in the top left photo. Sand the external rim profile if needed.

Cut a scroll chuck recess

Next, reposition the tool rest in front of the platter and true up the face with a roughing or spindle gouge or scraper. Next, lay out a recess in the bottom to fit your scroll chuck and cut the recess by defining the perimeter with a parting tool. Remove the waste in the recess with a spindle gouge or flat-nose scraper. Finally, cut the inside wall of the recess at an angle to match the jaws of your scroll chuck, using a dovetail scraper or a skew chisel laid on its side, as shown in the top right photo. Sand the bottom as needed, and turn off the lathe.

PLATTER/EDGE DETAILS

3½"

½"

7/8"

1 1/8"

5¼"

Mount the blank to the scroll chuck

Remove the face-plate/blank from the lathe and unscrew the faceplate from the blank. Then mount your scroll chuck on the lathe and fit the recess in the bottom of the platter over the jaws of the chuck. Tighten the chuck jaws to secure the blank as shown in the top left photo.

Turn the inside profile

Now you can turn the inside profile of the platter. A spindle gouge or fingernail gouge will make quick work of this, as shown in the middle photo. Make sure to stop frequently to check the depth of the interior as well as the thickness of the profile around the rim. If the wood is squirrelly and won't cut smoothly, try taking light cuts with a freshly burnished scraper.

Flatten the bottom

After you've shaped the inside profile, go back and use a square-nose scraper to flatten the bottom as shown in the bottom photo. Here again, light cuts are your best bet. Use a small metal straightedge or scrap of wood to check the platter bottom for flatness. When it's flat and you're satisfied with the profile, sand as needed. Then remove the platter from the scroll chuck.

Lay out the shaped edge

All that's left is to shape the edge. To do this, start by defining how much you'll remove. Using a compass is an excellent way to do this. Just set the width (in our case, $1/2$") to match the desired amount of lip you want to remove. Then hold the compass with the point butting up against the edge of the platter, as shown in the top photo. Next, simply slide the compass around the perimeter, and the pencil half of the compass will scribe a line defining the cut. Mark the start and stop points and any transitions as noted in the drawing on page 187.

Cut the edge

Now you can cut away the waste. A band saw or scroll saw will quickly remove this, as shown in the middle photo. You could also use a saber saw or a coping saw to cut away the waste. Just make sure to keep to the waste side of the line. You'll sand the edge to this line in the final step.

Sand the sawn edges

With the waste removed, use a drum sander to clean up the edges as shown in the bottom photo. You can fit the sander in a drill press as we did to guarantee a straight edge, or mount it in a portable drill and live with a little variation. After you've sanded up to the line, go back over the sanded edges with a piece of sandpaper to "break" the edges if desired. Then apply the finish of your choice.

INDEX

METRIC EQUIVALENCY CHART

Inches to millimeters and centimeters

inches	mm	cm	inches	cm	inches	cm
1/8	3	0.3	9	22.9	30	76.2
1/4	6	0.6	10	25.4	31	78.7
3/8	10	1.0	11	27.9	32	81.3
1/2	13	1.3	12	30.5	33	83.8
5/8	16	1.6	13	33.0	34	86.4
3/4	19	1.9	14	35.6	35	88.9
7/8	22	2.2	15	38.1	36	91.4
1	25	2.5	16	40.6	37	94.0
1 1/4	32	3.2	17	43.2	38	96.5
1 1/2	38	3.8	18	45.7	39	99.1
1 3/4	44	4.4	19	48.3	40	101.6
2	51	5.1	20	50.8	41	104.1
2 1/2	64	6.4	21	53.3	42	106.7
3	76	7.6	22	55.9	43	109.2
3 1/2	89	8.9	23	58.4	44	111.8
4	102	10.2	24	61.0	45	114.3
4 1/2	114	11.4	25	63.5	46	116.8
5	127	12.7	26	66.0	47	119.4
6	152	15.2	27	68.6	48	121.9
7	178	17.8	28	71.1	49	124.5
8	203	20.3	29	73.7	50	127.0

mm = millimeters   cm = centimeters

Photo Credits

Photos courtesy of Crown Tools (www.crownhandtools.ltd.uk): page 55 (bottom photo), page 145 (top right photo).

Photos courtesy of Delta Woodworking (www.deltawoodworking.com): page 10 (top photo), page 12 (bottom photo), page 31 (all photos), page 36 (middle photo), page 39 (bottom photos), page 42 (bottom photo).

Photos courtesy of Jet Tools (www.jettools.com): page 11 (top photo), page 12 (middle photo), page 27 (bottom photo), page 32 (left middle and bottom photos), page 33 (top photo), page 34 (all photos), page 35 (all photos), page 36 (bottom photo), page 37 (all photos).

Photos courtesy of Oneway Manufacturing (www.oneway.on.ca): page 8 (top photo), page 16 (bottom right photo), page 25 (top photo), page 27 (middle photo), page 30 (third photo from top), page 33 (middle photo), page 38 (middle and bottom photos).

Photos courtesy of Record Tools (www.recordpower.co.uk): page 26 (bottom photo), page 29 (middle left photo), page 30 (top two photos and bottom photo).

Photos courtesy of Robert Sorby Tools (www.robert-sorby.co.uk): page 38 (top photo), page 61 (bottom photo).

Photos courtesy of Teknatool (www.teknatool.com): page 9 (top photo), page 26 (top left photo), page 27 (top photo), page 28 (all photos).

Photos courtesy of Vega Woodworking (www.vegawoodworking.com): page 12 (top photo).